The Ancient Egyptian Roots of Christianity

Expanded Second Edition

Moustafa Gadalla

Tehuti Research Foundation
International Head Office: Greensboro, NC, U.S.A.

The Ancient Egyptian Roots of Christianity
Expanded Second Edition
by MOUSTAFA GADALLA

Published by:
Tehuti Research Foundation (formerly Bastet Publishing)
P.O. Box 39491
Greensboro, NC 27438 , U.S.A.

This second edition is a revised and enhanced edition of the same title that was published in 2007.

Publisher's Cataloging-in-Publication Data
Gadalla, Moustafa, 1944-
The Ancient Egyptian Roots of Christianity / Moustafa Gadalla. p. cm.

Includes bibliographical references.
Library of Congress Control Number: 2016900013

ISBN-13(pdf): 978-1-931446-75-4
ISBN-13(e-book): 978-1-931446-76-1
ISBN-13(pbk): 978-1-931446-77-8

1. Christianity—Origin. 2. Egypt in the Bible. 3. Egypt—Religion. 4. Jesus Christ—Historicity. 5. Tutankhamen, King of Egypt. 6. Egypt—History—To 640 A.D. 7. Pharaohs. I. Title.

BL2443.G35 2016
299.31–dc22

Updated 2018

CONTENTS

ABOUT THE AUTHOR

.Moustafa Gadalla is an Egyptian-American independent Egyptologist who was born in Cairo, Egypt in 1944. He holds a Bachelor of Science degree in civil engineering from Cairo University.

Gadalla is the author of twenty-two published internationally acclaimed books about the various aspects of the Ancient Egyptian history and civilization and its influences worldwide.

He is the Founder and Chairman of the Tehuti Research Foundation (https://www.egypt-tehuti.org)—an international, U.S.-based, non-profit organization, dedicated to Ancient Egyptian studies. He is also the Founder and Head of the online Egyptian Mystical University (https://www.EgyptianMysticalUniversity.org).

From his early childhood, Gadalla pursued his Ancient Egyptian roots with passion, through continuous study and research. Since 1990, he has dedicated and concentrated all his time to researching and writing

PREFACE

The very thing that is now called the Christian religion was already in existence in Ancient Egypt, long before the adoption of the New Testament. The British Egyptologist, Sir E. A. Wallis Budge, wrote in his book, *The Gods of the Egyptians* [1969]:

The new religion (Christianity) which was preached there by St. Mark and his immediate followers, in all essentials so closely resembled that which was the outcome of the worship of Osiris, Isis, and Horus.

The similarities, noted by Budge and everyone who has compared the Egyptian Osiris/Isis/Horus allegory to the Gospel story, are striking. Both accounts are practically the same, e.g. the supernatural conception, the divine birth, the struggles against the enemy in the wilderness, and the resurrection from the dead to eternal life. The main difference between the "two versions" is that the Gospel tale is considered historical and the Osiris/Isis/Horus cycle is an allegory. The spiritual message of the Ancient Egyptian Osiris/Isis/Horus allegory and the Christian revelation is exactly the same.

The British scholar A.N. Wilson pointed out in his book, *Jesus*:

The Jesus of History and the Christ of Faith are two separate beings, with very different stories. It is difficult enough to reconstruct the first, and in the attempt we are likely to do irreparable harm to the second.

This book will demonstrate that the "Jesus of History", the "Jesus of Faith", and the tenets of Christianity are all Ancient Egyptian. This will be done without causing any "irreparable harm" as per A.N. Wilson's concern, for two main reasons: Firstly, the truth must be told; Secondly, explaining Christian tenets via their original Ancient Egyptian contexts will enhance the idealism of Christianity.

This Expanded Version of the book consists of three parts to coincide with the terms of trinity—the Three that are Two that are One.

The first part demonstrates that the major biblical ancestors of the biblical Jesus are all Ancient Egyptian prominent individuals.

The second part demonstrates that the accounts of the "historical Jesus" are based entirely on the life and death of the Egyptian Pharaoh, Twt/Tut- Ankh-Amen.

The third part demonstrates that the "Jesus of Faith" and the Christian tenets are all Egyptian in origin—such as the essence of the teachings/message and the creation of the universe and man (according to the Book of Genesis), as well as the religious holidays.

There is an undeniable irony and a profound, deep, undeniable truth in Hosea's prophetic saying, *Out of Egypt have I called my Son*. A deep irony indeed.

Let us open our minds and review the available evidence; for the truth is a composite of different and complementary pieces of a puzzle. Let us put the pieces in the right location, time and order.

Moustafa Gadalla

STANDARDS AND TERMINOLOGY

---

1. The Ancient Egyptian word 'neter' and its feminine form 'netert' have been wrongly, and possibly intentionally, translated to 'god' and 'goddess' by almost all academicians. Neteru (plural of neter/netert) are the divine principles and functions of the One Supreme God.

2. You may find variations in writing the same Ancient Egyptian term, such as Amen/Amon/Amun or Pir/Per. This is because the vowels you see in translated Egyptian texts are only approximations of sounds, which are used by western Egyptologists to help them pronounce the Ancient Egyptian terms/words.

3. We will be using the most commonly recognized words for the English-speaking people that identify a neter/netert [god, goddess] or a pharaoh or a city, followed by other 'variations' of such a word/term.

It should be noted that the real names of the deities (gods, goddesses) were kept secret so as to guard the cosmic power of the deity. The Neteru were referred to by epithets that describe particular qualities, attributes and/or aspect(s) of their roles. Such applies to all common terms such as Isis, Osiris, Amun, Re, Horus, etc.

4. When using the Latin calendar, we will use the following terms:

BCE – Before Common Era. Also noted in other references as BC.

CE – Common Era. Also noted in other references as AD.

5. The term 'Baladi' will be used throughout this book to denote the present silent majority of Egyptians that adhere to the Ancient Egyptian traditions, with a thin exterior layer of Islam.[See *Ancient Egyptian Culture Revealed,* by Moustafa Gadalla, for detailed information.]

6. There were/are no Ancient Egyptian writings/texts that were categorized by the Egyptians themselves as "religious", "funerary", "sacred", etc. Western academia gave the Ancient Egyptian texts arbitrary names, such as the "Book of This" and the "Book of That", "divisions", "utterances", "spells", etc. Western academia even decided that a certain "Book" had a "Theban version" or "this or that time period version". After believing their own inventive creation, academia accused the Ancient Egyptians of making mistakes and missing portions of their writings?!!

For ease of reference, we will mention the common but arbitrary Western academic categorization of Ancient Egyptian texts, even though the Ancient Egyptians themselves never did.

MAP OF ANCIENT EGYPT

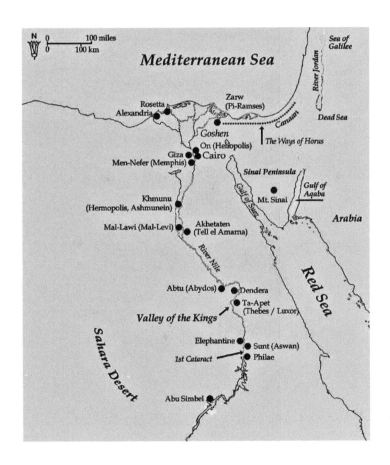

PART I : THE ANCESTORS
OF THE CHRIST KING

CHAPTER 1 : THE HISTORICAL CHRIST'S ROYAL ANCESTORS

1.1 SON OF THE HIGHEST

According to the Gospel of Luke, the angel Gabriel foretold of the Holy Mother and her future son:

> *He shall be great, and shall be called the Son of the Highest: and the Lord God shall give unto him the throne of his father David.* [Luke 1:32]

In Chapter 1 of the Gospel According to Matthew, the biblical Jesus is shown to be the descendant of:

1. King David
2. King Solomon
3. Moses

The intent of Part I of this book is to find the historicity of these three important biblical figures.

Over the last two thousand years, people have been searching for the historical existence/evidence of Jesus and other major biblical characters (Moses, David, Solomon, etc.). All these efforts have been fruitless because most people have accepted the biblical stories as historical events and searched for the evidence to support their pre-determined conclusions.

Common sense suggests the exact opposite direction in our search for the historical Jesus and other biblical characters. We should investigate what the historical evidence says about the biblical events, and not the other way around. We should not accept the biblical stories, figures and dates as historical fact without other corroborative evidence.

If we rationally review what happened, we will find that Egyptian historical evidence places certain Old Testament stories in logical settings. As such, many biblical stories, which are considered by many to be fairy tales, will become credible.

The Bible (which is notorious for stating the names of persons, sites, and water wells which in many cases have no impact on the story whatsoever) never named a Pharaoh or his residence when an event occurred.

While there is no historical evidence to support the biblical accounts of David, Solomon and Moses, there is abundant evidence to prove that:

> **Moses' life and religion match precisely with those of the Egyptian King Akhenaton (1367-1361 BCE).**
>
> **King David's war accounts match precisely with those of the Egyptian King Tuthomosis III (1490-1436 BCE).**
>
> **King Solomon's life and lack of wars match precisely with those of the Egyptian King Amenhotep III (1405-1367 BCE).**

The historical evidence is in conflict with the chronology of biblical characters, and no rational person can totally agree with the historicity of the Bible.

1.2 THE HISTORICITY OF THE BIBLE

The Biblical dates and ages are so erroneous that no logical person can take them seriously. The explanation that they may have attached a different meaning than we do to the word '*year*' does not explain errors in biblical chronology. Most scholars have now accepted the fact that the Bible is a blend of history and fiction, shaped by the political and religious disputes of ancient times.

In reading the Bible, one should consider the following facts:

– These stories were transferred by word of mouth over several centuries, before they were written down. As a result, biblical narration often confuses the names of places and people as well as the chronology of events.

– Upon writing the stories, the priests and the editors made their own "contributions" to the text that we have now.

– Translators have altered portions of the texts so as to comply with their '*standard of morality*'. Translation is difficult. One Hebrew word may need a dozen English words to explain its exact meaning.

1.3 MEANING OF KEY WORDS

When ancient writings are translated and/or interpreted incorrectly, one will find oneself on the wrong track in regard to relationships between individuals, their actual roles, and/or an erroneous chronology of events. In order to be able to understand and/or to realize these causes for some of the discrepancies in ancient writings, the following keywords show which have several meanings to each word.

Lord: This word could mean _God_, or _a person in a high position_. Taking this lingual fact into account will lead us to read many parts of the Bible in a different and interesting light.

Nurse: Two of the many meanings of this word are:

1. to suckle a child
2. to tend the sick

Mother: In the Middle East, it is not (and has not been) infrequent for women to suckle children who are not theirs. In this part of the world, the act of suckling a child will make the woman *a mother* to that child, and henceforth her <u>offspring will be *brothers and sisters* to the nursed (suckled) child</u>—which caused many to assume a number of incorrect blood relationships in the biblical accounts.

Sister: <u>Many ancient writings refer to wives as *sisters* and husbands as *brothers*</u>—which caused many to assume many incorrect blood relationships, in the biblical accounts.

1.4 PIECING THE PUZZLE

Throughout our daily lives, we make decisions and form opinions about events we have not witnessed personally, based on available evidence, experience and common sense.

Let us open our minds and review the available evidence; for the truth is the sum of a composite of different and complementary pieces of a puzzle. Let us put the pieces in the right location, time and order.

CHAPTER 2 : DAVID AND TWT HOMOSIS III

2.1 THE SAME NAME

Since the writings of the Ancient Egyptian language were limited to the consonants of words, the first segment of this Pharaoh's epithet was always with three consonants, as in *TWT*. For some mischievous reasons, the middle consonant letter was changed to the vowel *u* by some western Egyptologists. As such, this Pharaoh is commonly known as Twt Homosis (Tut Homosis) III.

When *Twt* is rendered in the Hebrew tongue, it becomes *Dwd*. When *Dwd* is pronounced phonetically it becomes *Dawood* which is the Hebrew name for *David*.

Is there any chance that the Egyptian warrior king was actually the biblical warrior King David? Let us study the accounts of the Egyptian King Twt Homosis (Tut Homosis) III and the biblical King David.

The life of the biblical David (that has no supporting historical evidence) can be divided into two parts:

- As a youth rising into prominence among his people.

- As a warrior king.

2.2 HIS YOUTH

Biblical Account

David, who the biblical theologians have arbitrarily assigned to the 10th century BCE for his time on earth, was the youngest son of Jesse. As a young boy he was a shepherd and a harpist. He was introduced to Saul, who appointed him as his armor bearer. Goliath, who was an armored and strong giant, came from the Philistine camp to intimidate the Hebrews by challenging them to a man-to-man contest. Goliath had a strong iron spear, a sword and a shield. Goliath asked the Israelites to choose an opponent and promised: *"If he be able to fight with me, and kill me, then we will be your servants."* David volunteered to fight Goliath but Saul tried to persuade him otherwise. Then David told Saul [according to I Samuel 17:34-37]:

> *Thy servant kept his father sheep, and there came a lion, and a bear, and took a lamb out of the flock: And I went out after him, and smote him, and delivered it out of his mouth: and when he rose against me, I caught him by his beard, and smote him, and slew him. Thy servant slew both the lion and the bear . . . . The Lord has delivered me out of the paw of the lion, and out of the paw of the bear, he will deliver me out of the hand of the Philistine.*

David refused to wear armor or carry a sword and went to face Goliath; David then knocked Goliath down with a stone from his sling and took Goliath's sword and cut off his head.

Historical Analysis of the Biblical Account

1. Many academicians have noted the similarities between the most famous Ancient Egyptian folktale *The Autobiography of Sinuhe* and the biblical account of David and Goliath. The Sinuhe folktale existed in many texts as far back as the 20th century BCE.

Therefore, it was developed a thousand years before the biblical account of David and Goliath was supposed to have occurred.

2. The Bible tells us that Goliath was a Philistine (which is the same as Palestinian). But when did these Philistines settle and establish themselves in Canaan? The archaeological evidence indicates that the Philistines became an established community only after the reign of Ramses III (c. 1182-1151 BCE), as per:

> a. The wall reliefs in Medinet Habu's temple in western Luxor (Thebes), which depict the mass invasion by the *Peoples of the Sea* of the coastal plain of Canaan, around 1174 BCE, which coincided with the Greek war against Troy. The wall inscriptions also indicate that the *Peoples of the Sea* consisted of fighters as well as refugees with their whole families. They were a combination of Peleset (which are Palestinians/Philistines—the word *Palestine* came from *Peleset*), Tjekker, Sheklesh, Danu and Weshesh. Ramses III defeated the invaders in a naval battle, but allowed the family refugees to settle in southwest Canaan.

> b. The Egyptian papyrus known as the *Harris Papyrus*, now located in the British Museum, states that Ramses III built a temple for **Amen/Amon** in Canaan after he defeated the invaders.

After the reign of Ramses III, Egypt lost its influence over Palestine, and the Philistines established themselves in the coastal plains of Canaan. Then they started expanding towards the Dead Sea and the River Jordan. It was at the same time that the Hebrews were trying to establish themselves in the area. As a result, both Philistines and Hebrews began fighting over the same piece of land.

Historically speaking, if David did do battle with the Philistines, then he could not have lived before the 12th century BCE, because that was when the mass migration of the coastal plain of Canaan by the Philistines took place. Therefore, <u>historical facts contradict the biblical time period</u> of the David and Goliath duel, which occurred during the first half of the 10th century, BCE.

Based on all the above, the story of David and Goliath is a fictional story which was inserted in the Bible in an attempt to enhance the biblical King David's trait as a hero and a warrior, and the events of the duel between David and Goliath were actually borrowed from the Egyptian literary work *The Autobiography of Sinuhe*.

Twt Homosis III As A Youth

It is most unfortunate that many people like to view the story of Hatshepsut/Twt Homosis III as an ancient contest between a man and a woman. Ancient Egyptians had the highest regard for women, and its society was based on matriarchal/matrilineal principles, practices, and traditions.

Twt Homosis II's father, namely Twt Homosis II (c. 1510–1490 BCE) married Hatshepsut and had a daughter, Neferure, from Hatshepsut. Twt Homosis II also had a son, Twthomosis III, by a concubine named Isis. Twt Homosis II died shortly after the birth of his son.

The line of the throne's inheritance, in Ancient Egypt, went through the eldest daughter; and whoever married her became the next pharaoh. But Neferure did not get married, so there was no husband to become Pharaoh.

Faced with the absence of an active and legitimate Pharaoh, the priesthood in Luxor (Thebes)—using divination—selected and declared Twt Homosis III as their Highest Priest (namely, the Pharaoh). Because of his young age, Queen Hatshepsut appointed herself as his guardian. A guardian is not recognized as the King. Therefore, in the chronology, Twt Homosis III is shown to begin his reign at 1490 BCE. Two years later, Hatshepsut began sharing kingship with Twt Homosis III, and dressed as a man. Twt Homosis III was kept powerless until Year 16 of the co-regency, when Neferure, the legal heiress, died.

After Neferure's death, Twt Homosis III gained increasing importance. When Hatshepsut died after 22 years of the co-regency, Twt Homosis III became the sole ruler of Egypt in 1468 BCE.

2.3 THE WARRIOR KING

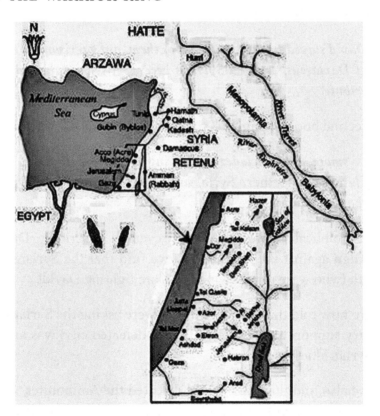

THE BIBLICAL WARRIOR KING

Shortly after the David and Goliath episode, David was suddenly transformed into a mighty warrior. The biblical accounts of the campaigns fought by David are described in the Second Book of Samuel. It shows an account of a series of wars in northern Palestine and Syria (up to the limits of the Mesopotamian river, the Euphrates) as well as Moab, to the east of the Dead Sea.

A few discrepancies in his biblical campaigns need to be discussed and clarified.

A. Confused Chronology

1. The Bible tells us that David defeated the confederate Syrian Kingdom, which was led by Hadadezer:

> **David slayed twenty thousand of them, put garrisons in Aram of Damascus, and the Syrians became his servants and paid tribute.**

The second book of Samuel (8:3) specifically tells us that David

> **... smote also Hadadezer ... King of Zobath** (located near Hamath in northern Syria)**, as he went to recover his border at the river Euphrates.**

2. Two biblical chapters later, however, in describing David's campaign against the Ammonites, we find that the Syrians and Zobath (who were totally wiped out) are fighting David!

We are now told that the Ammonites were asking the Syrians for military support and that Zobath (the defeated city) was among the Syrian allies!

We are also told that after David defeated the Ammonites' allies, they fled and sought refuge in their city, Rabbah (present-day Amman, the capital city of Jordan), and that David's army returned to besiege Rabbah:

- **This situation is impossible, if Zobath had already been defeated and David had established garrisons in**

Syria. Geographically and logically, these two events must have taken place chronologically in reverse order of that described in the biblical account.

B. Confused City-Names

1. Rabbah – is present-day Amman, the capital city of Jordan. The Bible claims that David conquered Rabbah after a long siege. However, no archaeological evidence was ever found to support that claim.

The biblical editor made a mistake in naming *Rabbah* as the city, besieged and attacked by David. The correct name is *Megiddo*.

The Bible itself disputes the validity of the Rabbah story, as shown in the four points below:

a. The military importance of Megiddo and its legend as an international battleground is reflected in John [Revelation, 16:16]. *Armageddon* (**Har Meggiddon**, *the Mount of Megiddo*) is the site where, at the end of days, all the kings of the world will fight the ultimate battle against the forces of God.

b. In the second book of Samuel (10:2), we are told that David took the city of Rabbah, whose king was Hanun. Seven chapters later, we find Rabbah independent under its king, Shobi, who felt pity on David and his followers because they were

> **hungry and weary, and thirsty in the wilderness.** [II Samuel, 17:28-9]

Rabbah was a minor insignificant location at that time.

c. Solomon, David's successor, raised a levy so as to

> **build the wall of Megiddo.** [I Kings, 9:15]

d. Megiddo is also mentioned as one of Solomon's possessions in I Kings, 4:12.

2. Zobath – No traces of a locality with this name have been found in either Syria or Canaan at the supposed time of David (10th century BCE) or Twt Homosis III (15th century BCE). Zobath was mistaken for the city of Qadesh, the northern Syrian stronghold, on the River Orontes.

The Egyptian Warrior King

When Twt Homosis III became the sole ruler of Egypt after the death of Hatshepsut, four decades had passed without a major Egyptian military campaign in western Asia. During this period, the Syrian King of Qadesh led a coalition in a war against Egypt's Asiatic allies, whom the Egyptians helped in defeating their enemies during the reign of Twt Homosis I (c. 1528-1510 BCE).

In response to the aggression against Egypt's Asiatic allies, Twt Homosis III led a total of 17 campaigns in western Asia over the next 20 years. The daily events of these wars fought by Twt Homosis III, were recorded by the scribes who accompanied the army on its campaigns. These records are to be found in the *Annals*, a 223-line document that covers the inside of the walls enclosing the corridor surrounding the granite holy of hollies, which Twt Homosis III built at the Karnak temple.

> **The historical details of the wars fought by the Warrior King Twt Homosis III, as posted in the Karnak temple, match precisely the biblical accounts of the wars fought by the Warrior King David, in the second book of Samuel, except for the discrepancies in the chronology of a single event and the two city names, mentioned earlier.**

The common denominator of the events at the biblically-named Rabbah and the Egyptian named Megiddo, as evident from both the war annals of Twt Homosis III and the biblical account of David's campaigns, are:

- The king fought against a major fortified city in Canaan that was aided by a Syrian confederation led by a king of one Syrian city;

- The king's army defeated the coalition near the city gates and the enemy sought sanctuary within its fortified walls;

- The king's army surrounded the city for a long time before they attacked and took it; and

- After the defeat of the Syrian confederation at (Rabbah/ Megiddo), the main Syrian city continued to threaten the king. The king and his army therefore conquered that Syrian city and went further to regain the borders at the River Euphrates. He then erected a stela in celebration of his triumph.

Historical and archaeological evidence confirms that these military campaigns occurred during the reign of Twt Homosis III. There is no evidence to support the biblical account that these events occurred five centuries later, at the alleged time of the biblical David in the first half of the 10th century BCE.

CHAPTER 3 : SOLOMON AND AMENHOTEP III

3.1 GENERAL

The evidence points to Amenhotep III, as being the historical figure of the person identified in the Old Testament as Solomon. This evidence is described below.

Thirty-two years after the reign of Twt Homosis III, Amenhotep III became the King of Egypt.

King	Length of Reign	Dates
Twt Homosis III (David)	54	1490-1436 BCE
Amenhotep II	23	1436-1413 BCE
Twt Homosis IV	8	1413-1405 BCE
Amenhotep III (Solomon)	38	1405-1367 BCE

Egypt was the universal leader of the known world. Amenhotep III later became known as *King of kings, ruler of rulers ...*

Amenhotep III's reign was almost entirely peaceful except for a minor military operation along Egypt's southern frontier, during Year 5 of his reign. The name Solomon means *safety or peace.*

Solomon, according to the Old Testament, followed David to the throne at Jerusalem. Biblical theologians have arbitrarily assigned c. 965-925 BCE as the dates of Solomon's 40-year reign. The peaceful conditions of Amenhotep III's reign were also attributed to the biblical Solomon.

There is no historical record of a ruler named Solomon at any time. Furthermore, both the Old Testament and the Talmud agree that Solomon was not the king's original name. According to II Samuel 12:25, at the time of his birth, Nathan gave Solomon the name of Jedidiah, meaning *because of the Lord or by the word of the Lord*.

3.2 CORONATION OF THE KING

Amenhotep III, as the King of Egypt, was regarded as the son of the deity. This is an exclusively Ancient Egyptian concept, applying to all their kings.

The idea of kingship, originally foreign to the Hebrews, was introduced into Hebrew theology from the time of David onward. In their case, as in Egyptian tradition, the king is regarded as the son of the deity. Jehovah tells King David in Psalms 2:7, **Thou art my son; this day have I begotten thee**. He also says of Solomon, **I will be his father, and he shall be my son** [II Samuel, 7:14]

Anointing the king was an Ancient Egyptian custom that has been recorded in Ancient Egypt since at least 2700 BCE.

According to the Bible, David ordered Solomon to be anointed **King over Israel** [I Kings, 1:34]. Like the Egyptians, the Hebrew Lord began referring to his kingly son as His anointed. [Psalms, 2:2, 18:50, 20:6] The Ancient Egyptian word for *the anointed one* is **MeSSeH**. In the Hebrew tongue, the Egyptian **S** is pronounced **SH**; and as such, it becomes **MeSHeH**.

[More details about this subject in Part II of this book.]

3.3 THE KING'S EGYPTIAN WIFE

Amenhotep III married Sitamun, the eldest daughter of Twt Homosis IV. Since the line of royal descent was through the eldest daughter, Amenhotep III became the Pharaoh.

After marrying the Egyptian Sitamun to inherit the throne, he subsequently married Tiye.

Similarly, the biblical Solomon

> *made affinity with Pharaoh king of Egypt, and took Pharaoh's daughter, and brought her into the city of David.* **[I Kings, 3:1]**

The pharaoh whose daughter was married to Solomon was (as is the case, in the Bible, with all Egyptian pharaohs) never named. The pharaoh in question, however, is said to have

> *gone up, and taken Gezer, and burnt it with fire, and slain the Canaanites that dwelt in the city, and given it for a present unto his daughter, Solomon's wife.* **[I Kings, 9:16]**

This biblical verse has no historical validity.

None of the Egyptian kings who lived during the alleged reign of Solomon [21st Dynasty] were involved in military campaigns in western Asia.

3.4 THE GREAT BUILDER

Amenhotep III was reputed to be a great builder. The construction activities at the sites mentioned below, in I Kings, 9:15, are very similar to the archaeological findings of works completed during the reign of the Egyptian Pharaoh Amenhotep III.

Likewise, the biblical Solomon is reputed to have been a master builder. He built **the house of the Lord, and his own house, and Millo, and the wall of Jerusalem, and Hazer, and Megiddo, and Gezer [I Kings, 9:15]** and numerous other building activities.

No archaeological findings in the named building sites bore any inscription that identified a king named Solomon, or anything else related to his alleged kingdom.

To summarize: there is historical and archaeological evidence of building during the reign of Amenhotep III that matches those ascribed to Solomon. However, none of them are dated to the 10th century BCE, the alleged time when the biblical Solomon ruled.

Let us review the construction activities at the sites mentioned above in I Kings, 9:15, in their same order.

1. The Temples

The Bible tells us that Solomon built a temple on Mount Moriah, north of Jerusalem. The site is now occupied by the Dome of the Rock mosque and therefore no excavation can be carried out to search for this temple.

There are, however, some remarkable similarities between this biblically described temple and the vanished commemorative temple of Amenhotep III in western Luxor (Thebes).

Even though no remains of this commemorative temple have been found, two colossal statues of the seated king, just under 70 ft. (20 m) tall, stood at the front of the temple and still exist in western Luxor (Thebes).

The two statues are comparable to the two pillars of the biblical Solomon's temple. The two Egyptian statues have names, like the mentioned biblical pillars.

On a stela that came from this temple, we find the original inscription of Amenhotep III, in which he describes the temple as:

> **an everlasting fortress of sandstone, embellished with gold throughout, its floor shining with silver and all its doorways with electrum. It is extended with statues of**

granite, of quartzite and precious stones, fashioned to last forever.

Similarly, much precious material was also used in the biblically-described Solomon temple.

Amenhotep III is known to have built many other temples, both in Egypt and in Canaanite cities. Archaeological evidence supports the belief that several of the biblically-described Solomonic temples were built in Canaan during the reign of Amenhotep III.

2. The Millo

The British archaeologist Kathleen Kenyon was able, in 1961, to uncover the remains of the Millo (filling), which was utilized in the widening of the ground level below the ancient fortress of Jerusalem. She was able to date the first construction of the Millo to the 14th century BCE—the time of Amenhotep III.

No evidence was found to relate the Millo to the 10th century BCE, during the biblical Solomon's alleged reign.

3. Sites of Fortifications

[Location map in the prior chapter of this book.]

There is archaeological evidence of fortifications at Hazor, Megiddo and Gezer. All three cities are contained in the list of western Asiatic cities that were conquered by Twt Homosis III. The resulting destruction from these wars was followed by rebuilding 50 years later during the reign of Amenhotep III. Egyptian objects, including a cartouche of Amenhotep III, were found in the strata belonging to this period—indicative of the rebuilding activities.

None of the archaeological items found bore any inscription that identified a king named Solomon, or anything else related to his supposed kingdom. Furthermore, the Old Testament did not give us any description matching any of the archaeological findings.

To summarize, there is historical and archaeological evidence of building during the reign of Amenhotep III that matches those ascribed to Solomon. However, none of them are dated to the 10th century BCE, the alleged time when Solomon ruled.

3.5 THE WISDOM OF THE KING

Amenhotep III was reputed to be a wise king.

Solomon is described in the Bible as being very wise:

> *King Solomon exceeded all the kings of the earth for riches and for wisdom.* **[I Kings, 10:23]**

The reasons given for such wisdom brings forth more similarities between Solomon and Amenhotep III.

The Bible attributes the author of the Books of Hebrew's wisdom and poetry to Solomon. Where did all this wisdom literature come from? The answer is summarized in John Bright's finding:

That parts of the Proverbs are based on the Egyptian Maxims of Amenemope (Amenhotep III) is well known.

This is yet another confirmation that Solomon and Amenhotep III are one and the same person.

3.6 DIFFERENT ERAS

Despite the hard work of biblical theologians, historians and archaeologists, no single piece of evidence has been found to support the period of the supposed United Monarchy of David and Solomon. Scholars have been confused by the biblical chronology which presents David and Solomon as having belonged to the period following both the Exodus and the settlement in the "Promised Land".

Many of these biblical events occurred four to five centuries earlier than what the Old Testament would have us believe. Both Twt Homosis III, the historical King David, and Amenhotep III, the Biblical Solomon, belonged to the 18th Dynasty of Egypt.

The biblical scribes were so bold as to manipulate historical events. They wrote their accounts in a historical fashion, but there is no historical evidence to support their manipulated accounts.

CHAPTER 4 : MOSES AND AKHENATON

4.1 MONOTHEISM AND MONOMANIA

The Ancient Egyptians believed in One God who was self-produced, self-existent, immortal, invisible, eternal, omniscient, almighty, etc. This One God was represented through the functions and attributes of "His" domain. These attributes were called the **neteru** (pronounced *net-er-u,* masculine singular: **neter**; feminine singular: **netert**). In other words, the ALL (**neteru**) are the One.

When we ask, "Who is God?", we are really asking, "What is God?". A mere name or noun does not tell us anything. One can only define "God" through the multitude of "His" attributes/ qualities/powers/actions. To know "God" is to know the numerous qualities of "God". Far from being a primitive, polytheistic form, this is the highest expression of monotheistic mysticism.

The Ancient Egyptians utilized pictorial symbols to represent the divine attributes and actions. As the saying goes, "a picture is worth a thousand words." As a result, the figures of Isis, Osiris,Horus, Mut, etc., became the symbols of such attributes/functions/forces/energies, and were never intended to be looked upon as real personages.

In Egyptian symbolism, the precise role of the **neteru** (gods/goddesses) is revealed in many ways: by dress, headdress, crown, feather, animal, plant, color, position, size, gesture, sacred object (e.g., flail, scepter, staff, ankh), etc. A chosen symbol represents that function or principle on all levels simultaneously—from the simplest, most obvious physical manifestation of that function to the most abstract and metaphysical. This symbolic language represents a wealth of physical, physiological, psychological and spiritual data in the presented symbols.

Those who lack understanding of the Egyptian monotheistic mysticism are quick to pronounce Akhenaton as *the first monotheist*. Akhenaton glorified one Egyptian neter (god), namely **Aton**—the disk of the sun—over and above all the other neteru (gods/goddesses).

Likewise, the God of Moses declared:

> ... *against all the gods of Egypt I will execute judgment; I am the Lord.* [Exodus, 12:12]

The evidence points to Akhenaton as being the historical figure of the person identified in the Old Testament as Moses. This evidence is described below.

4.2 MONOTHEIST OR MONOTYPIC

In Egypt, the king always represented the divine in man. Akhenaton thought that it was he, Akhenaton the man, who was Divine. It is only the Divine that is both male and female, and the so-called "Amarna art" depicts Akhenaton as both male and female. There are portraits that depict Akhenaton with female breasts, but other portraits do not include this feature. The most compelling portrait is found in the Akhenaton room at the Egyptian Museum in Cairo—one of the nude colossi shows the king as being unmistakably androgynous. Written into this astonishing art is a pervasive deliberate sexual symbolism that depicts him as simultaneously both a man and a woman. His statue shows a unisex human representing the Perfect One—who is neither male or female—as none other than God.

4.3 FREUD AND MOSES

Sigmund Freud, the Jewish father of psychoanalysis, was intensely interested in Jewish history. He later wrote a book called *Moses and Monotheism*. Sigmund Freud argued that Moses was an Egyptian, a follower of Akhenaton, who later led the Jews out of Egypt.

Even though the Bible (in Exodus, 2:10) tells us that Moses' Egyptian adopted mother called him *Moshe* because, she said, *I drew him out of the water*, Freud demonstrated that Moshe had a different meaning. In fact, the name **Moshui** is the Hebrew name which means *one who has been drawn out*. It was then Freud's conclusion that the name of the Jewish leader was not of Hebrew origin, but rather from an Egyptian origin.

Mos is part of many compound Ancient Egyptian names such as **Ptah-mos** and **Tuth-mos**. We also find some examples of the word *mos* being used on its own as a personal pronoun and which means *rightful person*. Such practice was common during the 18th Dynasty.

Many generations later and in a different country, a biblical editor, who may not have had any knowledge of Moses' original name, attempted to provide a *Hebrew explanation* of the name. It is also possible that the biblical editor was trying to remove any possible link between Moses and his position as a Pharaoh of Egypt.

Sigmund Freud's findings (that Moses was not a Hebrew, but an Egyptian) upset some and outraged others. But as the decades have rolled along, Freud's concept has sunk into the consciousness of Western thought, and at the beginning of the new millennium (of our common era), it no longer seems outrageous.

Next, we shall draw distinct parallels between the historical

Ancient Egyptian Pharaoh Akhenaton and the biblical accounts of Moses.

4.4 ATON WORSHIP

There were very many **neteru** (gods, goddesses) in Egypt. **Aton** was among this multitude of deities, and was not a new idea, but was introduced by Akhenaton. Archaeological evidence of **Aton** is found in Ancient Egyptian texts dating to the time of the 12th Dynasty, 600 years before Akhenaton was born.

The image of **Aton** is presented as a sun disk with its rays ending in human hands.

Akhenaton exalted **Aton** over and above the other aspects/powers/**neteru** of the One Supreme God.

Adonai in Hebrew means *my Lord.* The last two letters *'ai'* of the word is a Hebrew pronoun meaning *'my'* or *'mine'* and signifying possession. '*Adon*,' meaning *Lord,* was correctly noted by Sigmund Freud as the Hebrew word for the Egyptian **Aton/Aten.** As the Egyptian '**t**' becomes '*d*' in the Hebrew tongue, *Adon* is the Hebrew equivalent of the Egyptian **Aton**. Thus, *Adon* and **Aton/Aten** are one and the same.

• • •

The Ancient Egyptians had numerous hymns to all their deities—including **Aton**. One of these hymns to **Aton**—often attributed to Akhenaton—is a mirror image of Psalm 104. Here are both versions for you to compare:

<u>Hymn to the Aton</u>

> *The cattle are content in their pasture, the trees and plants are green, the birds fly from their nests. Their wings are raised in praise of your soul. The goats leap on their feet. All flying and fluttering things live when you shine for them. Likewise*

the boats race up and down the river, and every way is open, because you have appeared. The fish in the river leap before your face. Your rays go to the depth of the sea.

Psalm 104

He causeth the grass to grow for the cattle, and the herb for the service of man: that he may bring forth food out of the earth: and wine that maketh glad the heart of man and oil to make his face shine, and bread which strengtheneth man's heart. The trees of the Lord are full of sap: the cedars of Lebanon which he hath planted: where the birds make their nests: as for the stork, the fir trees are her house. The high hills are a refuge for the wild goats; and the rocks for the conies.... So is this great and wide sea, wherein are things creeping innumerable, both great and small beasts. There go the ships.

The similarity of sequence and of images in both compositions is too striking to be a coincidence. As such, many believe that the earlier Egyptian hymn must have been known to the later Hebrew writer.

• • •

Akhenaton chose the Heliopolitan solar form of the Egyptian temple to be used as the place for the worship of the **Aton.**

Likewise, Moses was the first person to introduce a temple into Israelite worship when he created the tabernacle in Sinai.

• • •

Akhenaton continued the Egyptian practice of a holy boat, which was usually kept in the temple.

Moses also adopted the ark, where the Pentateuch scrolls were kept (Exodus, 25:10). The ark is respected as the second holiest part of the Jewish temple after the Pentateuch itself.

. . .

Akhenaton continued the Egyptian priesthood system and associated rituals.

There was no Israelite priesthood before the time of Moses. Rituals and worship of the newly established Hebrew priesthood were similar to those during the time of Akhenaton. Moses arranged the priesthood in two main levels: the high priests and the ordinary priests. Instructions were issued to them about their specific garments, purification, anointment and how best to go about fulfilling the duties of their offices.

. . .

Across the Nile from Tell-el Amarna, there is the city of **Mallawi** (Mal-Levi), which literally means *The City of the Levites*. The Levites held priestly positions with Akhenaton at Amarna. Likewise, the Levites held priestly positions with Moses, according to the Bible.

Akhenaton's two highest priestly officials were:

> 1. **Meryre II**, who was the High Priest of the **Aton** at the Amarna temple.

> 2. **Panehesy**, who was the Chief Servitor of the **Aton** at Akhenaton's temple in Amarna.

Likewise, Moses' two highest priestly officials were:

> 1. *Merari*, who is described in Genesis, 46:11 as one of the sons of Levi. The Egyptian equivalent of **Merari** is **Meryre**.

> 2. *Phinehas*, who was the son of Eleazar and grandson of Aaron according to Exodus, 6:25. His name in the Talmud is *Pinhas*. The Egyptian equivalent of his name is **Panehesy**.

It is therefore evident that we are dealing with the same high officials who served Akhenaton at Amarna and then accompanied him to Sinai afterwards: Yet another confirmation that Moses and Akhenaton are one and the same.

4.5 THE RULER

Akhenaton's 18-year reign was mostly a co-regency. He reigned the first twelve years in conjunction with his father, Amenhotep III. It was very probable that the last few years of his reign was a co-regency with his brother Semenkhkare. Both his participation and outright rule of Egypt can be divided into four stages:

1. Early Co-Regency Rule

When Amenhotep III's health began to deteriorate, Akhenaton's mother Tiye's power increased correspondingly. In order to ensure her son's inheritance of the throne, she arranged for him to marry his half-sister, Nefertiti, who was the daughter of Amenhotep III by Sitamun, the legitimate heiress. It is Nefertiti who is recognized in the Bible as Miriam, *Moses' sister*—which is a common mistake in translation between a wife and a sister. [See the end of Chapter 1 of this book for the explanation.]

In order to bypass the legitimate process of the power transfer between succeeding pharaohs, Tiye prompted her husband, Amenhotep III, to appoint Amenhotep IV (Akhenaton) as his co-regent. As such, Akhenaton evaded the coronation rituals that can only be performed by the priests.

Akhenaton became a co-regent in or about Year 28 of Amenhotep III. At about Year 33, he transferred his residence to Tell el-Amarna, 200 miles north of Luxor (Thebes). His reign had two groups of dated inscriptions. One was related to the Luxor (Thebes) residence, which started at Year 28 of Amenhotep III. The other one was related to the Amarna residence. A correspondence in date, year by year, between the two groups of inscriptions can be easily established. For example, Year 28 of Amenhotep III equals Year 1 of Amenhotep IV. Year 33 of Amenhotep III is equal to Year 6 of Amenhotep IV, etc. Amenhotep III died in his Year 38, which was Akhenaton's Year 12.

In his fifth year of co-regency, Amenhotep IV changed his name to Akhenaton in honor of the **Aton**.

Because of the hostile climate that Akhenaton created, he left Luxor (Thebes) with Amenhotep III and went to reside at Tell el-Amarna (200 miles [330 km] north of Luxor). Akhenaton named his new residence *Akhetaton,* meaning *the city of the horizon of the Aton*. This area is also called Amarna/Tell el-Amarna. The name is, however, derived from the name in the second cartouche of Akhenaton's god; namely. *Im-r-n.*

Amram, or Imran, was the name given in the Bible to Moses' father, and it is precisely the same name Akhenaten gave to his *father*, the Aton.

Yet another confirmation that Moses and Akhenaton are one and the same.

The co-regency ended when his father died in Akhenaton's Year 12.

2. Sole Ruler

Akhenaton became sole ruler after Amenhotep III died in Year 12 of Akhenaton. He failed his duties as an Ancient Egyptian pharaoh, to continuously perform the necessary rituals for the proper relationship and communication with the neteru (the powers of the universe) in order to maintain the welfare of the state and insure the fertility of the earth so that it may bring forth sustenance. The Ancient Egyptian pharaoh was never meant to be a ruler or a leader of an army. However, throughout his reign,

Akhenaton relied completely on the army's support for protection.

3. Late Co-Regency Rule

With the temples inactive, the pressure mounted on Akhenaton, who ignored his main function as the high official priest of all temples and shrines. As a last resort (or as a ploy), Akhenaton, in his Year 15, was forced to install his brother, Semenkhkare, as his co-regent at Luxor. This action only delayed the inevitable outcome.

Semenkhkare left Amarna for Luxor (Thebes), where he reversed Akhenaton's hostile actions and began a reconciliation process with the priests there.

In his Year 17, Akhenaton suddenly disappeared. At or about the same time, Semenkhkare died suddenly. The co-regency of Akhenaton and Semenkhkare was succeeded by the young prince, Twt-Ankh-Amen.

In his Year 17, Akhenaton may have been warned by his uncle, Aye, of a threat on his life. He abdicated and fled to Sinai, with his followers. The sudden departure is evident in the lack of burial, or even of sarcophagi, in any of the nobles' or royal tombs of Akhetaton.

Although Sinai was part of Egypt from the early days of Egyptian history, there was no established governing authority there, because of its sparse and nomadic population.

The sudden disappearance of Akhenaton is echoed in the biblical story of Moses when he escaped to Sinai, after he slew an Egyptian. The account of how Moses slew an Egyptian may have been mentioned in the Amarna Tablets. Among these tablets is a letter, sent from AbdKhiba, King of Jerusalem, to Akhenaton, in which

AbdKhiba accuses Akhenaton of not punishing some Hebrews who killed two Egyptian officials:

> ... the Khabiru (Hebrews) are seizing the towns of the king ... Turbazu has been slain in the very gate of Zilu (Zarw), yet the king holds back ... Yaptih-Hadad has been slain in the very gate of Zilu, yet the king holds back.

Did the final blow to Akhenaton's reign lie in letting the Hebrews get away with two murders?

4. King Without Power—"Co-regency" with Twt-Ankh-Aton

Even though Akhenaton abdicated and fled from the scene, he was still regarded as the legitimate ruler. As long as he was alive, the pharaoh was regarded as being the legitimate pharaoh.

Akhenaton would not let go of his powers and as a result he made (through co-regency) his 10-year-old son Twt-Ankh-Aton the official Pharaoh. Being of a minor age, this allowed Akhenaton, his father, to be in control for four more years, and during this time the boy King was still called Twt-Ankh-**Aton**.

This "co-regency" ended four years later, Year 21 of Akhenaton, when Aye (Akhenaton's uncle) became the de facto guardian of the young King. Subsequently, the young King abandoned the **Aton** (at least officially) by changing his name from Twt-Ankh-**Aton** to Twt-Ankh-**Amen**.

At this point in time, the exclusiveness of **Aton** as the "only/ prime god/neter" ended and Akhenaton, who was still alive in Sinai, was king no more.

4.6 THE EXILE

No evidence has ever been found regarding the date of Akhenaton's death. Akhenaton's city, including his tomb, was substantially destroyed. However, archaeologists were able to reconstruct, from many small fragments, Akhenaton's sarcophagus, which is the outermost of a series of coffins that would protect his mummy. The presence of the inner coffins would indicate burial. This absence indicates otherwise. No fragments of the inner coffers were ever found. Additionally, the actual canopic jars that would have contained the viscera of the deceased have never been found. The absence of these jars, or their fragments, from Akhenaton's tomb is more strong evidence that he was never buried there.

According to the Talmud, when Moses was 18, he fled Egypt after killing an Egyptian. He then became a soldier and fought on the side of the King of *Ethiopia*. After the King won, Moses became very popular. As a result, when the king died, Moses was appointed as their new king.

The Talmud tells us that (like Akhenaton) the legitimacy of Moses as King stirred up the society. As a result, the Talmud account says, that even though the people loved and wanted him, Moses resigned voluntarily, and departed from their land. The people of Ethiopia bestowed great honors upon him.

There are many similarities between The Talmud story of Moses and the Akhenaton story at Amarna:

> 1. Moses was elevated to the post of king for some time before going to Sinai. Akhenaton likewise.

> 2. The Talmud reference to *Ethiopia*, which is described as being a city, was mistaken for the Amarna location. It is also possible that *Ethiopia* was mistaken for utopia.

The account of the reign of Moses in the Talmud indicates that he resigned his post, but did not die at that time. The logical conclusion is that he died and was buried outside Egypt proper—in the Egyptian outpost at Moab—as shown next.

4.7 THE DEATH OF MOSES/AKHENATON

The account in the Old Testament of the failure of Moses to reach the *Promised Land*, his death and his burial in an unmarked grave is another curious episode.

We are told initially that when his followers complained of thirst, Moses used his rod to smite a rock and bring forth water. It was called *"the water of Meribah"*—a location in the north-center of Sinai, south of Canaan. It was this action that would later haunt him.

Some time later, when the Israelites were camped on the banks of the Jordan near Jericho and opposite Canaan, Moses learned, according to the *Book of Deuteronomy*, that he was to be denied the opportunity to cross the river, no matter how hard he pleaded:

> *I pray thee, let me go over, and see the good land that is beyond Jordan, that goodly mountain, and Lebanon.*
> *... the Lord said ... speak no more unto me of this matter ...*
> *... thou shalt not go over this Jordan.* [Deuteronomy 3:25-7]

Later in the *Book of Deuteronomy*, we have an account of the actual death of Moses. The Lord said to him:

> *Get thee up into this mountain Abarim, unto Mount Nebo, which is in the land of Moab'* (the borders between Sinai and eastern Jordan) *'that is over against Jericho; and be-hold the land of Canaan, which I give unto the children of Israel for a possession: And die in the mount ... Because ye trespassed against me among the children of Israel at the waters of Meribah-Kadesh, in the wilderness of Zin*
> *... thou shalt not go thither unto the land which I give the chil-dren of Israel.* [Deuteronomy 32:49-52]

It is irrational to believe that God would punish Moses for providing water for his thirsty people. It is more logical to

believe that trespassing onto Egyptian water wells may cause the Egyptian authorities to punish him for such a violation—as confirmed by the Egyptian records.

The Egyptian Pharaoh Seti I (C. 1333-1304 BCE) received a message about the chaos in Sinai:

> *The Shasu enemies are plotting rebellion. Their tribal leaders are gathered in one place, standing on the foothills of Khor (a general term for Palestine and Syria), and they are engaged in turmoil and uproar. Each of them is killing his fellow.*

In response, Seti I led his army promptly to Sinai. Seti I's war scenes, on the exterior north wall of the great Hypostyle Hall at Karnak, show that his first campaign against the Shasu (the tribes in Sinai) occurred when they attacked the small settlements along the Road of Horus, the ancient highway connecting Egypt with western Asia. This took place immediately after the Exodus from Egypt, possibly when they trespassed to obtain water from Egyptian settlements along that road. Seti I chased them as far as the city of Canaan, Gaza and, as a result, killed their leader, Moses, and many of his followers. Subsequently, they fled into Sinai for what the Old Testament calls *"the forty years of wandering"*.

To prove that the Shasu and the Israelites are the same group of people, scholars studied:

1. The Shasu appearance in Sinai, in Year 1 of Seti I's reign, and their subsequent movements over the following 100 years. This information was provided from ancient Egyptian records.

2. The biblical accounts of the Exodus and their subsequent movements over 100 years.

Scholars concluded that both of them followed the same route at exactly the same time sequence; i.e. the Shasu and the Israelites are one and the same group of people.

The Talmud provides a different account than the Old Testament of how Moses died. There is a Talmudic reference to a confrontation and a struggle between Moses and the '*Angel of Death*' on the Mount before he died. This had persuaded some biblical theologians scholars to believe that Moses was killed.

It seems more likely that Moses, using his royal scepter (symbol of authority), entered one or more of the Egyptian settlements along Horus Road to obtain water from their wells. Such actions were reported to Seti I, who reacted by chasing the Shasu, here identified as the Israelites, into northern Sinai. If these Talmudic references to the death of Moses are correct, it must have been there that Seti I confronted Moses/ Akhenaton before the latter's death.

PART II : THE HISTORICAL CHRIST KING

CHAPTER 5 : JESUS AND HISTORY

5.1 THE JESUS OF HISTORY

- The Gospels of Matthew, Mark, Luke and John, written several generations after the time of the events they describe, state that Jesus was born in Judaea (which lies between the Mediterranean and the Jordan–Dead Sea–Arab depression) during the time of Herod the Great (37-4 BCE), and that his condemnation to death, suffering and crucifixion occurred when Judaea became a Roman province with Pontius Pilate as its procurator (26-36 CE).

- Mark was not an eyewitness to the events that he described in the Bible. Neither were Matthew, Luke or John, who followed him later. Despite the existence of many Gospels of Christ in the early history of the Church, the Council of Trent in 1546 only accepted the four included in the New Testament—those of Matthew, Mark, Luke and John.

=> **The "common" story, by the four Gospels, of the life and death of Jesus has no corroborative evidence to support it. Only its continuous repetition to us has made it appear as an established historical fact.**

5.2 THE HISTORICAL ABSENCE AND GOSPELS' PROMINENCE

Despite the Gospels' story of the biblical Jesus, there has never been: 1) any archaeological evidence to corroborate it; 2) any

Roman record that can bear witness, directly or indirectly, to the Gospel story of Jesus; 3) any corroboration to the Gospels' story in the writings of Jewish authors living at that period in Jerusalem or Alexandria.

There were some attempts to add some references to Jesus of the Gospels—at a later date—to some of the writings of Jewish authors. However such attempts have been exposed as forgeries, produced either by Christians who wished to validate the historicity of their Lord, or enemies of Christianity who wished to attack the religion.

The usual response to the historical absence of the Biblical Jesus is that he was an ordinary man and not an important figure to warrant any attention or place in history. The Bible itself provides the contrary evidence to such a discredited claim.

A. Herod, the King of Judea, as per the following biblical verses, knew of Jesus

1. When Jesus was born

   ... wise men from the East came to Jerusalem, saying, "Where is he who has been born King of the Jews?"... [Matthew, 2:1-2]

2. King Herod was told of a prophecy that the Christ was to be born in Bethlehem:

   ... for from you [Bethlehem] shall come a ruler who will govern my people Israel. [Matthew, 2:6]

3. Upon hearing the above prophecy, Herod was distressed by the news of his birth and therefore Joseph was ordered by the angel of the Lord to:

   Rise, take the child and his mother, and flee to Egypt, and remain there till I tell you; for Herod is about to search for the child, to destroy him. [Matthew, 2:13]

4. Herod was so distressed that he:

sent for and killed all the male children in Bethlehem and in all that region who were two years old and under. [Matthew, 2:16]

5. After Jesus was sentenced to death by the Jewish hierarchy, they handed him over to Pilate who:

... when he learned that he belonged to Herod's jurisdiction, he sent him over to Herod, who was himself in Jerusalem at the time. [Luke, 23:7]

Pilate later told the chief priests:

I did not find this man guilty of any of your charges against him; neither did Herod, for he sent him back to us. [Luke, 23:14-16]

B. The Bible tells us that Jesus was a very important figure:

1. Wise men from different nations came to offer homage to him, as per Matthew, 2:1-2.

2. *He was born <u>to be King</u>,* as per Matthew, 2:2.

3. *He was born <u>to be a ruler</u>:*

... For from you shall come <u>a ruler</u> ... [Matthew, 2:6]

4. He was born to **govern:**

... <u>who will govern</u> my people Israel [Matthew, 2:6]

5. He ruled as a King as per the overwhelming shown in a later chapter of this book , *The Divided Kingdom.*

C. Jesus was very visible, attracting crowds from all over the region and causing a lot of commotion, as per the following biblical verses:

1. The joyous crowds are welcoming their king. So they took branches of palm trees and went out to meet him, crying, *"Hosanna! Blessed is he who comes in the name of the Lord, even the King of Israel!"* [John, 12:13]

**An Egyptian scene strikingly similar to the biblical verse
(Palm Sunday)**

2. *And he went about all Galilee teaching in their synagogue, and preaching the gospel ... so his fame spread throughout all Syria, and they brought him all the sick ... And great crowds followed him from Galilee and ... from beyond the Jordan.* [Matthew, 4:23-25]

3. *And those who ate were about five thousand men, besides women and children.* [Matthew, 14:21]

4. *... a great multitude from Galilee followed; also from Judea and Jerusalem and Id-u-Me'a and from beyond the Jordan and from about Tyre and Si'don a great multitude, hearing all that he did, came to him.* [Mark, 3:7-8]

5. Here is a crowd of more than 9,000 people:

When I broke the five loaves for the five thousand ... And the seven for the four thousand ... [Mark, 8:19-20]

5.3 MOSES AND JESUS OF THE SAME ERA

The Jewish writings (which never corroborated the Gospels' story of Jesus) wrote of a much earlier *Jesus*.

The Talmudic rabbis do not relate the *earlier* Jesus to the time of Herod or Pontius Pilate. They do, however, refer to an *earlier* Jesus who was killed by a priest named Pinhas. The Talmud is quite specific: *"Pinhas ... killed him [Jesus]"* [b. Sanh., 106b]. Pinhas (Phinehas in the Old Testament) was the priest, the son of Eleazar, the son of Aaron, who is identified in the Book of Numbers as a contemporary of Moses.

The Talmudic references to Pinhas/Phinehas and Jesus were ignored because they show Jesus living at the same time as Moses did.

The tendency for the faithful and those who grew accustomed to the story of the Gospels is to outright reject the Talmudic references to Jesus being of the same era as Moses. Yet corroborating evidence from the early fathers of the Church, as well as the Bible itself, concur with the Talmudic writings.

The Bible itself confirms that Jesus lived fourteen centuries earlier than had been thought. Note the event described in the Gospels of Matthew, Mark and Luke about the meeting of Jesus and Moses, at the time of what is known as his Transfiguration:

> *And after six days Jesus taketh with him Peter, and James, and John, and leadeth them up into a high mountain apart by themselves: and he was transfigured before them. And his raiment became shining, exceeding white as snow; so as no fuller on earth can white them. And they appeared unto them Elias (Elijah) with Moses: and they were talking with Jesus. And Peter answered and said to Jesus, Master, it is good for us to be here: and let us make three tabernacles; one for thee, and one for Moses, and one for Elias ...* [Mark, 9:2-5]

John, after using a reference to Isaiah to report some of the activities of Jesus, goes on to say:

> *Isaiah said this because he saw his glory, and spoke of him.* [John, 12:41]

John is stating that Isaiah saw the glory of Jesus. However, *Jesus is said to have achieved glory only after his death and Resurrection:*

> *... God, that raised him up from the dead and gave him glory ...* [I Peter, 1:21]

and also:

> *... the sufferings of Christ and the glory that should follow ...* [I Peter, 1:11]

=>**To summarize: John acknowledged that Christ lived and died before the time of Isaiah's writings (who lived during the second half of the 8th century BCE)**

5.4 JESUS: THE GNOSTIC NAZARENE

It is an error to think that *Jesus the Nazarene* means Jesus from a city named Nazareth located in Galilee.

The name *Nazareth* is **not found** in:

- The Book of Acts
- The letters of the Apostles
- Any book of the Old Testament
- The Talmud

– The whole works of the Jewish historian Josephus, who was himself given command in Galilee at the time of the Jewish revolt against the Romans in 66 CE.

– The English version of the New Testament always and incorrectly translated the word *Nazarene* as of *Nazareth*.

– The Talmud never mentions that Jesus was a Galilean or came from the city of Nazareth. The Tal-mud refers to him as being a Nazarene indicating a religious sect, not a geographical location, as per [b. Sanh., 107b]:

Jesus the Nazarene who practiced magic in Egypt.

The Nazarenes were one of many Gnostic sects (seekers of knowledge through spiritual experience). Hebrew Jews, to this day, use the term *Nazarene* for Christians. *Nazarenes* signifies a religious sect, as per the following biblical verses:

1. *"For we have found this man (Paul) a pestilent fellow, an agitator among all the Jews throughout the world, and a ring-leader of the sect of the Nazarenes."* [Acts, 24:5]

2. *"But this I admit to you, that according to the Way, which they call a sect, I worship the God of our fathers, believing everything laid down by the law or written in the prophets ..."* [Acts, 24:14]

5.5 CONCLUSIONS

– There is not a shred of contemporary evidence to support the New Testament story of the birth, life or death of Jesus.

However, there is a wealth of evidence proving that the historical Jesus lived many centuries earlier.

– The New Testament, the Old Testament and the Talmud place Jesus and Moses in the same era.

With no historical support for a biblical Jesus, a Jesus of history should be examined in the Ancient Egyptian historical context.

The next chapters will establish the identity of the historical figure of Jesus as being Tutankhamen/Twtankhamen (Twt-Ankh-Amen). A key element in the analysis will be the confirmation of the Ancient Egyptian evidence that both the biblical Moses (historical Akhenaton) and the biblical Jesus (historical Twt-Ankh-Amen) were of the same turbulent era.

We will prove that the two are from the one and same era, by matching:

1. Their recognized epithets.

2. Identities of their personal relationships (father, mother, birth, consort/wife).

3. Each's role and activities (in life) as a king and a peacemaker.

4. Their violent deaths.

CHAPTER 6 : HIS EPITHETS

The biblical Jesus and Twt-Ankh-Amen share many similarities, including their variety of "names". Here is a sampling:

6.1 THE LIVING IMAGE OF THE LORD

Twt-Ankh-Amen shares this very important epithet with the biblical Jesus.

Twt's birth name was Twt-Ankh-**Aton**. Twt-Ankh means *the Living Image*. **Aton** signifies the Egyptian neter(god), meaning *Lord*. Since the Hebrews tend to pronounce the letter *t* as *d*, the Lord is called *Adon*.

As such, <u>Twt/Tut's birth name</u> therefore means *the living image of the Lord*.

6.2 CHRIST

The English word *Christ* comes from the "Greek" *Christos*—a corrupted Ancient Egyptian word with the consonants H.RST. Since the Greeks cannot pronounce the letter H. (the 8th letter, which they pronounce *eta*), they substituted its sound with the letters Ch. The consonants of the name Christ are H.RST, which means **HeRu** (Horus), Son of ST (**auST**/Isis). Twt/Tut-Ankh-Amen's role as an Egyptian Pharaoh was (symbolically) the son of a Virgin Mother—**Auset** (Isis).

6.3 MESSIAH

The English word *Messiah* originated also from the Hebrew and Aramic *Mashih*, which in its form as a verb *MeSHeH* means to *anoint*. This word is of Egyptian origin, where **MeSSeH** [the letter *s* in Egyptian is equivalent to *sh* in Hebrew and Aramaic] signified the ritual of anointing Ancient Egyptian Kings (including Twt-Ankh-Amen) with the fat of crocodiles, as was the tradition with all kings in Ancient Egypt since at least 2700 BCE. Anointing was a ritual of the coronation of the Egyptian King. Thus *the Christ/Messiah means the anointed one*, who is *the king*.

As such, Twt/Tut-Ankh-Amen, as the Egyptian Pharaoh, was also the Messiah.

The concept of the birth of the Messiah without sexual intercourse originated in Ancient Egypt. Isis is said to have conceived her son Horus after her husband Osiris' death. The cosmic force responsible for her impregnation was MeSSeH. the crocodile star, as per Spell 148 of the *Coffin Texts*:

> **The crocodile star (MeSSeH) strikes ... Isis wakes pregnant with the seed of Osiris— namely Horus.**

6.4 JESUS/JOSHUA

The names *Joshua* (*Ye-ho-shua* in Hebrew) and *Jesus* (*Ye-shua* in its short form) have the same meaning, which is: *Yahweh (the Lord) is salvation*. The Greek text of the Bible reports both names as *Jesus*. The *King James Bible* and many of the early Church Fathers of the 2nd and 3rd centuries CE refer to *Joshua* and *Jesus* as one and the same person.

Twt-Ankh-Amen—as an Egyptian Pharaoh—was the Lord of Salvation, representing Osiris on earth. [Read more about these similarities in the next section of this book.]

6.5 EMMANUAL/IMMANUEL

The evangelist, Matthew, regarded Immanuel as another name for Jesus: *"... they shall call his name Immanuel, which being interpreted is 'God with us'"*. [1:23]

Immanuel could be interpreted in two ways, by dividing the word into its basic elements:

1. Imma-nu (with us) and El (Elohim, God) i.e. *God with us.*

2. Imman-u (his Amun) and El (is God) i.e. *His Amun is God.*

The first interpretation of Immanuel was intentionally highlighted in the Bible in order to hide the fact that it is the second interpretation which was intended, i.e.: His **Amen is God**. [Read more details in a later chapter .]

This latter interpretation is echoed in King Twt's changing his name from Twt-Ankh-**Aton** to Twt-Ankh-**Amen**.

Immanuel's relationship to **Amen** is found in:

[Revelations, 3:14] *And to the angel of the church in La-o-di-ce-a write: 'The words of the Amen, the faithful and true witness, the beginning of God's creation.*

and [2 Corinthians, 1:19,20] *For the Son of God, Jesus Christ, ... we utter the Amen through him, to the glory of God.*

The meaning and role of Amen in Ancient Egypt system is exactly as described in the above biblical verses. [More details follow,in a later chapter about Genesis.]

6.6 BEN PANDIRA (SON OF GOD)

In some Talmudic passages, Jesus is named *Ben Pandira*, meaning the son of Pandira.

Pandira is a corrupt Hebrew form of an Ancient Egyptian term. The Hebrew **Pa-ndi-ra**, in its original form, is **Pa-ntr-ra** (pronounced *Pa-neter-ra*). Ben means *son*. Ben Pandira, as such, means *Son of God* [Son of the **neter** (god) **Ra**]. All Egyptian kings since ca. 3000 BCE had the title **Son of Ra**.

Thus, *Ben Pandira* (Son of **Ra**) identifies Jesus as an Egyptian king. The title, *Son of Ra*, is engraved on Twt/Tut-Ankh-Amen's stela, which was found in the Karnak Temple in 1905.

CHAPTER 7 : THE DIVINE MAN

7.1 THE BIBLICAL JESUS—THE DIVINE SON

– The Gospels' claim that Jesus was born in Bethlehem during the Roman Era has never been proven by any shred of historical evidence.

– The birth of Jesus is not mentioned in New Testament writings of the 1st century CE; only the later Gospel writers refer to it. Two of the four Gospels refer to his birth, yet they differ in their details.

– By the year 200 CE, the Church issued the Creed that Jesus Christ was *"conceived by the Holy Ghost"* and *"born of the Virgin Mary"*.

– The virgin concept evolved further when the Council of Trullo in 692 CE declared that Mary, the mother of Jesus was *ever-virgin*.

– The virgin idea reached its peak in the writings of St. Thomas Aquinas in the 13th century. The church endorsed his writing which said that:

> *Because she conceived Christ without the defilement of sin, and without the stain of sexual mingling, therefore did she bring him forth without pain, without violation of her virginal integrity, without detriment to the purity of her maidenhood.*

=> The Virgin Birth, as such, became a historical (not spiritual) *fact* by the Church.

The holy (virgin) birth of the Egyptian king is a recurring theme in temples and writings throughout Ancient Egypt. In Ancient Egypt, divine birth was looked upon as an aspect of spiritual purity. Although the child was regarded spiritually as the son of the deity, this did not exclude a human father or the sexual relationship between the parents. In symbolic terms, the spirit of the deity used the physical body of the queen to produce the child. In Christian belief, however, no human father is involved: the mother is a virgin, and the child is conceived by the Holy Spirit without any sexual relationship.

The immaculate conception of the king is documented in scenes as well as texts found in many places, such as on the north wall of the central colonnade of Queen Hatshepsut's mortuary temple at Deir el Bahari, as well as at the Luxor Temple. In the Luxor Temple at the *Birth Chamber*, as it is called by classical Egyptologists, we find the scene of the spiritual conception and birth of the king. The reliefs on the west wall depict a scene with many similarities to the familiar Christian's Immaculate Conception. The king was a royal, conscientious man with divine potential. The Egyptian king is therefore considered to be the spiritual son of God: the son of the **neteru**, the divine principles.

=> The Egyptian model story of Isis, Osiris, and Horus represents the idea of virgin birth in its original spiritual and purest form [more details in the next part of this book].

7.2 TWT-ANKH-AMEN—THE DIVINE SON

Twt-Ankh-Amen was born in the city of Amarna, the chosen residence of his father, Akhenaton.

Amarna was named after Amran (or Imran), which is the

name of Akhenaton's god (father) and which is also the name given in the Bible for Moses' father.

Across the Nile from Tell-el Amarna there is the city of **Mallawi** (Mal-Levi), which literally means *The City of the Levites*. The Levites, according to the Bible, held priestly positions with Moses, when actually they held the very same positions with Akhenaton (Twt's father).

=> **This is another indication that Jesus and Moses were of the same era.**

7.3 TWT-ANKH-AMEN'S FATHER

His father was Akhenaton, as per the evidence presented in answering the following questions:

1. Was Twt-Ankh-Amen the son or brother of Akhenaton?

- Akhenaton and his father Amenhotep III had a co-regency, for twelve years, before Akhenaton ruled alone. According to a shirt found in Twt/Tut-Ankh-Amen's tomb, he was born during Akhenaton's Year 7 at Amarna. The shirt evidence provides two conclusions:

  a. Since the date on the shirt refers to Akhenaton, therefore and in accordance with the ancient Egyptian practices, Akhenaton was his father.

  b. Akhenaton's Year 7 would make Twt/Tut-Ankh-Amen ten years of age when he came to the throne and nineteen when he died. These dates are confirmed by anatomical examination of his body, as well as by dated objects found in his tomb.

2. Was Akhenaton's mother, Queen Tiye, the mother or grandmother of Twt-Ankh-Amen?

- As stated earlier, Twt-Ankh-Amen was born in Year 7 of his father Akhenaton. During the co-regency of Amenhotep III and Akhenaton, Year 7 of Akhenaton corresponds to Year 33 of Amenhotep III. At such a time, Queen Tiye was about 41 years old. Two years earlier she had given birth to a daughter, Baketaton.

So, hypothetically Queen Tiye could have been able to give birth to a son at age 41. However, the evidence found in her steward Huya's tomb indicate that Tiye's first visit to Amarna was during or after Akhenaton's Year 10 – three years after Twt-Ankh-Amen's birth.

The above mentioned shirt indicates a birth in Akhenaton's Year 7 and at Amarna, i.e. when and where Tiye was not present.

Therefore the logical conclusion is that Akhenaton was the father of Twt-Ankh-Amen, and Queen Tiye was the grandmother.

7.4 THE BIBLICAL JESUS' FATHER

– Only two of the four Gospels tell us that Joseph the carpenter was Jesus' shadow father. The Bible tells us that this Joseph was a descendent of King David. Notwithstanding all these clear statements, the Bible insists that Jesus, who is not the biological son of this Joseph, was the descendant of King David!

– This Joseph, *the carpenter*, disappears from the scene before the supposed ministry of Christ. Nothing is said about his fate!

– Jesus is of a royal descendant, as per Matthew 1:1: ***"Jesus Christ, the son*** [descendant] ***of (King) David."***

– The order of the Messianic Banquet (Passover meal) said that God would *"beget"* the Davidic Messiah. The second book of Samuel 7:13-14 affirms the same point:

I will establish the throne of his kingdom for ever. I will be his father, and he shall be my son.

The New Testament (Hebrews, 1:5) affirms the same idea of the Messiah as the Son of God, *"begotten"* of the Father.

– Other points related to Jesus' (Divine) father, such as the immaculate conception were discussed earlier in this chapter.

=> The relationship between the biblical Jesus and his father (The Divine) is exactly the same concept as in the Ancient Egyptian model allegory of Osiris, Isis, and Horus. [More information will be presented in a later chapters, *The Ancient Egyptian/Christian Holy Families*, and in the chapter *The Way of Horus/Christ*.]

7.5 TWT-ANKH-AMEN'S MOTHER

Since Akhenaton fathered Twt/Tut-Ankh-Amen (as proven earlier), his wife, Nefertiti, must have been the mother of Twt-Ankh-Amen.

Before the birth of Twt-Ankh-Amen, Nefertiti had three daughters, and then another three afterwards. From the archaeological findings at Amarna's northern residence, it can be concluded that Nefertiti remained there with her son, Twt-Ankh-Amen, before and after he began his reign. This also ratifies the maternal relationship.

7.6 THE BIBLICAL JESUS' MOTHER

The biblical name of Jesus' mother is Mary. The name **Mary** is given to many women in the Bible. The two closest women to Jesus were called **Mary:** his mother and **Mary** Magdalene.

The origin of the name **Mary** lies in Ancient Egypt, where the written word **Mr** (the vowels a and y were added by modern scholars to help pronounce the ancient languages) means *the beloved*. The name **Mary/Mery** is one of the most repeated words in Ancient Egyptian texts. It was used as an adjective (epithet) before names of people, **neteru** (gods), etc. This epithet was also applied to many of the Egyptian royal family members, including his mother, Nefertiti, and his wife, Ankhsenpa-aton.

The Mother Mary has been described, in the Talmud, as *"the descendant of princes and rulers"* [b. Sanh. 106a]. This description can only fit Nefertiti, the biblical Madonna.

=> The familiar Christian scene of the Virgin and Child is a copy of a common and abundant Ancient Egyptian statue—such as the 6th century BCE statue of Isis and her son Horus, now in the Turin Museum. It was such a statue that inspired the 15th century painter Masaccio in his presentation of The Virgin and Child. We can easily find one or several such Ancient Egyptian statues in museums throughout the world.

Isis' role in the Egyptian Model Story and the story of the Virgin Mary are strikingly similar, for both were able to conceive without male impregnation. Horus was conceived and born after the death of Isis' husband and, as such, Isis was revered as the **Virgin Mother**.

The ideal of virginity was a cornerstone of the Ancient Egyptian traditions. Ancient Egyptian women are depicted wearing a vulture headdress. The choice of the vulture for this particular feminine role is because:

a. The vulture is supposed to be particularly zealous in caring for its young.

b. There is no physical sexual contact between male and female vultures. <u>The female vulture gets impregnated by exposing herself to receive the male seeds carried by the winds without physical contact. The vulture is therefore a symbol of virgin birth.</u>

7.7 TWT-ANKH-AMEN'S CONSORT

- Ankhsenpa-**Aton** was, as evident from her name, a worshiper of **Aton** (*Adonai* in Hebrew).

- She was the third daughter of the reigning queen Nefertiti. The Amarna kings did not follow the Ancient Egyptian rule that only the eldest daughter inherits the throne, but twisted such traditions. The eldest daughter of Nefertiti married Semenkhare (Akhenaton's brother)—who preceded Twt-Ankh-Amen—and the second daughter died earlier.

- As stated earlier, she was called Mary/Mery which is an Egyptian epithet meaning *beloved*.

- Twt-Ankh-Aton/Amen and Ankhsenpa-Aton are shown together in several scenes, always in a relaxed, romantic mode. One can sense her love for Twt-Ankh-Amen, similar to Mary Magdalene's love for the biblical Jesus.

- Alabaster ointment jars were found in the Twt-Ankh-Amen tomb. On the back of his throne, his wife is shown anointing him with perfume exactly as the evangelists described Mary Magdalene anointing the biblical Jesus.

As his wife and queen, she was the only person who could attend his funerary rites, witness the priests announce his Resurrection, and inform his disciples of the news. She is shown doing all that in Twt-Ankh-Amen's tomb.

7.8 THE BIBLICAL JESUS' CONSORT

Mary, a name given to most women in the Bible, meant *beloved* in Ancient Egypt. The term *Magdalene* has been explained as belonging to or from the city of Magdala, an unidentified location on the western shore of the Sea of Galilee. The word **migdol** means a *tower*. A city named Migdol was located on Horus Road, leading from Egypt to Gaza.

This Mary is described in the Bible as being a person who is emotionally related to Jesus.

> *There came a woman having an alabaster box of ointment of spikenard very precious; and she brake the box, and poured it on his head.* [Mark, 14:3]

> *And [she] stood at his feet behind him weeping, and began to wash his feet with tears, and did wipe them with the hairs of her head, and kissed his feet, and anointed them with the ointment.* [Luke, 7:38]

As a result of this close relationship, "Mary Magdalene" became one of those who followed the biblical Jesus until after his death. She was very close to him. After his death, she waited at his temporary burial place. She was the one who the biblical Jesus talked to after his resurrection:

> *Jesus saith unto her, Mary. She turned herself, and saith unto him, Rabboni; which is to say, Master. Jesus saith unto her, Touch me not; for I am not yet ascended to my Father: but go to my brethren, and say unto them, I ascend unto my Father, and your Father; and to my God, and your God.* [John, 20:16-17]

This biblical description is depicted in Twt-Ankh-Amen's tomb.

CHAPTER 8 : THE DIVIDED KINGDOM

8.1 THE BIBLICAL JESUS—THE KING

To portray the biblical Jesus as an ordinary man of a humble family background is to contradict the overwhelming evidence in the Bible itself that he was a monarch with power and authority. Here are some biblical references:

1. The Bible describes him as of royal blood, born "King of the Jews". The Bible tells us that when Jesus was born,

> *wise men from the East came to Jerusalem, saying, "Where is he who has been born King of the Jews?"* [Matthew, 2:2-3]

2. The Bible tells us that Herod, the King of Judea, was told of a prophecy that the biblical Jesus was to become,

> *... a ruler who will govern my people Israel.* [Matthew, 2:6]

The biblical description of "a ruler to govern" leaves no doubt regarding his prominent role.

3. He was a man of authority:

> *And when Jesus finished these sayings, the crowds were astonished at his teachings, for he taught them as one*

who had authority, and not as their scribes. [Matthew, 7:28-29]

4. He was addressed by the crowd as *"Lord"* on numerous occasions, signifying a person in a high position.

5. He showed his authority when he commanded his disciples to bring somebody else's ass and colt because:

> *<u>The Lord has need of them.</u>" "... Jesus sent two disciples, saying to them, "Go into the village opposite you, and immediately you will find an ass tied, and a colt with her; untie them and bring them to me. If any one says anything to you, you shall say, 'The Lord has need of them'* [Matthew, 21:1-3]

6. The next biblical verses describe his role as the King of the Jews:

> *"Tell the daughter of Zion, Behold, your king is coming to you, humble, and mounted on an ass, and on a colt, the foal of an ass."*[Matthew, 21:5]

Also a very similar verse is stated in John, 12:13-15.

7. The only question asked to him indicates that he was the King:

> *"And Pilate asked him, "Are you the King of the Jews?" And he answered him, "You have said so."* [Mark, 15:2]

Very similar verses are stated in Matthew, 27:11 and Luke, 23:3-4.

8. A short time later he again was referred to as the King:

Hail, King of the Jews! [**Matthew, 27:29**]

9. Another reference to him as the King:

And they began to salute him, "Hail, King of the Jews!" [**Mark, 15:18**]

10. The charge against him that caused his execution was being the "King of the Jews":

And over his head they put the charge against him, which read, "This is Jesus the King of the Jews." [**Matthew, 27:37**]

Also:

And the inscription of the charge against him read, "The King of the Jews." [**Mark, 15:26**]

11. More references to him as the King:

He is the King of Israel ... [**Matthew, 27:42**]

Let the Christ, the King of Israel ... [**Mark, 15:32**]

... and saying: "If you are the King of the Jews, save yourself!" There was also an inscription over him, "This is the King of the Jews." [**Luke, 23:37-38**]

12. Here, again, he is called the King of the Jews:

And he answered them, "Do you want me to release for you the King of the Jews?" [**Mark, 15:9**]

13. Another reference to him as the King:

> *And Pilate again said to them, "Then what shall I do with the man whom you call the King of the Jews?"* [Mark, 15:12]

14. He was the descendent of kings:

> *Jesus Christ, the son* [meaning descendant]*of (King) David* [Matthew, 1:1]

15. The Bible clearly states that Jesus inherited the throne of King David:

> *... and the Lord God will give to him the throne of his father* [meaning his ancestor] *David.* [Luke, 1:32]

16. He was addressed by ordinary people as *"Son of David"* on numerous occasions throughout the Bible, which provides additional evidence that the historical Christ was of royal descent.

– The Talmud agrees that:

1. The historical Jesus was of royal descent, describing his mother as:

> *... the descendant of princes and rulers.* [b. Sanh, 106a]

2. The historical Jesus was in (from) Egypt:

> *Jesus the Nazarene who practiced magic in Egypt.* [b. Sanh., 107b]

3. Jesus was a King:

> *... It seems that the King is crucified.* [T. Sanh., 9.7]

8.2 TWT-ANKH-AMEN—THE KING

Twt-Ankh-Amen, like Jesus, can also be described as: Son of the Highest seated upon the throne of his father (*father* here means *ancestor*).

The young king was ten years of age when he started his rule in 1361 BCE as a co-regent with his exiled father, Akhenaton. The following are the highlights of his nine year reign:

> For four years he continued to live at Amarna, and during this time period, he was still called Twt-ankh-**Aton**. Nefertiti continued to live with her children in the northern residence at Amarna. She was still referred to as the *Great King's Wife*, indicating that Akhenaton was still alive and influential.

> During his Year 4, the co-regency with Akhenaton ended and Aye (Akhenaton's uncle) became the de facto guardian of the young king. They then moved his residence from Amarna to Memphis, southwest of modern Cairo. At that time, he changed his name from Twt-Ankh-**Aton** to Twt-Ankh-**Amen**, and his queen's name changed from Ankhsenpa-**Aton** to Ankhsenpa-**Amen**. The change was in recognition of **Amon/Amen**.

> The change of names did not reflect a change of heart, because he still adhered completely to the **Aton** worship, as evident from his recovered throne. At the top center of his throne, one can see the symbol of the **Aton** with its extending rays, giving the ankh (the Egyptian key of life) to Twt-Ankh-Amen and his wife. Two cartouches of Twtankhamen are shown on the throne. One of these cartouches proves that he used this throne after he had changed his name.

Restoration of buildings and grounds of the temples—neglected during the reign of Akhenaton—were carried out. A stele of Twt-Ankh-Amen at Karnak includes the official work order:

> *Now His Majesty appeared as king at a time when the temples of the neteru from Elephantine as far as the Delta marshes had fallen into ruin, and their shrines become neglected. They had turned into mounds overgrown [with] weeds, and it seemed that their sanctuaries had never existed.*

A text on a lion of red granite in the British Museum refers to Twt-Ankh-Amen:

> *He restored the monuments of his [ancestor] Amenhotep III.*

=> This sounds very much like the complaint that Jesus is said to have made about the conditions of the temple at Jerusalem.

8.3 TWT-ANKH-AMEN—DIVIDED KINGDOM

In both cases of Twt/Tut-Ankh-Amen and the biblical Jesus, the evidence indicates a deep division in the kingdom. Akhenaton, King Twt's father, antagonized the populous. After a few years of his tyranny, Akhenaton was forced to abdicate, and went into hiding with his followers to Sinai.

In his Year 9, Twt-Ankh-Amen, accompanied by Aye, went to

Sinai to try to urge Akhenaton and his followers to return to Egypt. He wanted them to live in harmony with people of different beliefs, whom they regarded as enemies. His repeated message was reconciliation, forgiveness and tolerance. Unlike his father, he accepted that not everyone had the same perception of God and not everyone worshiped him in the same way. His message was: *Live and let live.*

Instead of his pleas being accepted, he was accused of betraying his faith and was killed.

8.4 THE BIBLICAL JESUS—DIVIDED KINGDOM

Similarly, the biblical Jesus went solely to bring back the disgruntled Adonai/Aton followers:

> *These twelve (disciples) Jesus sent out, charging them, "Go nowhere among the Gentiles, and enter no town of the Samaritans, but go rather to the lost sheep of the house of Israel."* [Matthew, 10:5-6]

The biblical Jesus, who was referred to numerous times as the *King of the Jews*, never abandoned his Jewish beliefs, as confirmed in Matthew, 5:17:

> *Think not that I have come to abolish the law and the prophets, I have come not to abolish them but to fulfill them.*

Here are some of the clear biblical references to the division in his kingdom as he addressed the Jews:

> 1. ... *he said to them, "Every kingdom divided against itself is laid waste, and no city or house divided against itself will stand; and if Satan casts out Satan, he is divided against himself; how then will his kingdom stand?* [Matthew, 12:25-26]
>
> 2. *If a kingdom is divided against itself, that kingdom cannot*

stand. And if a house is divided against itself, that house will not be able to stand. [Mark, 3:24-25]

3.*But he, knowing their thoughts, said to them, "Every kingdom divided against itself is laid waste, and house falls upon house."*[Luke, 11:17]

Like Twt/Tut, his message was also reconciliation, forgiveness and tolerance. His message was very clear in his Sermon on the Mount: portions of which are mentioned herein.

1. *Blessed are the peacemakers, for they shall be called Sons of God.* [Matthew, 5:9]

2. *Judge not, and you will not be judged; condemn not, and you will not be condemned; forgive, and you will be forgiven; give, and it will be given to you; good measure, pressed down, shaken together, running over, will be put into your lap. For the measure you give will be the measure you get back.* [Luke, 6:37-38]

Similarly, his pleas were not accepted. Instead he was accused of betraying his faith—and was killed.

CHAPTER 9 : DEATH IN THE WILDERNESS

9.1 TWT-ANKH-AMEN

The violent nature of Twt/Tut-Ankh-Amen's death is evident from the condition of his mummy. An extensive examination of Twt's mummy, including the use of x-rays, was carried out in 1968 by Professor R.G. Harrison, the late Professor of Anatomy at Liverpool University, and A.B. Abdalla, Professor of Anatomy at Cairo University. The following are excerpts from their report:

> *... the mummy was not in one piece. The head and neck were separated from the rest of the body, and the limbs had been detached from the torso...*
> *... the limbs were broken in many places as well as being detached from the body. The right arm had been broken at the elbow, the upper arm being separated from the forearm and*

hand... The left arm was broken at the elbow, and in addition
at the wrist... The left leg was broken at the knee
... The heads of the right humerus [bone of the upper arm] and
both femora [thigh bone] had been broken off the remains of the
bone ...
... The head and neck had been distracted from the torso at the
.joint between the seventh cervical and first thoracic vertebrae.
"The tissues of the face are contracted on the skull ...
"The teeth are tightly clenched together ...
"The radiographs of the thorax confirmed the tact that the ster-
num and most of the ribs on the front of the chest had been
removed."'

The examination failed to find any evidence of disease as the cause of death, and it is clear from the state of his remains that Twt/Tut-Ankh-Amun did not die of natural causes but must have been exposed to severe physical torture, then hanged.

The funerary mask of Twt-Ankh-Amen, the best likeness of a pharaoh ever found, shows the suffering eyes of the young King, at his death.

Howard Carter, who discovered the tomb of Twt-Ankh-Amen in 1922, provided numerous observations regarding the contents of the tomb, which provided additional striking similarities between Twt-Tut-Ankh-Amen and the biblical Jesus. Carter reported that he found many items in Twt-Ankh-Amen's tomb that linked them *"to later Christian beliefs and practices"*, such as:

a. His scepter, which was used in conjunction with offerings. It contains this text:

The Beautiful God, beloved, dazzling of face like the Aton
when it shines ... Twt-Ankh-Amen.

The text is very similar to the biblical accounts <u>of the</u>

Transfiguration of Jesus and his *"shining face"* on the Mount shortly before he died.

b. Fruits and seeds of Christ-thorn, a tree like a haw-thorn native to Ancient Egypt, used for food or medicine and also said to have had some religious significance.

These thorny shrubs were said to have been used for Christ's crown of thorns:

And the soldiers plaited a crown of thorns, and put it on his head ... [John, 19:2]

c. Two ritual robes, which Carter identified as the *"same priestly dalmatic worn by Christian deacons and bishops."*

The botanical evidence found in the tomb shows that Twt/Tut-Ankh-Amen must have died in the spring and was buried 70 days later, the time required for the mummification and other subsequent processes before the actual burial. Spring blossoms and fruits were found in wreaths, on top of the second and third coffins, dried out before use. The wreath on the third coffin included the mandrake fruits, sliced in half, which were dried out before they were sewn on to the wreath. Additionally, the blue water lily used in these wreaths does not bloom until the summer.

Twt-Ankh-Amen most probably died in April, the same time as the biblical Christ's death. The time of death coincides with the Jewish holiday of Passover (and later the Christian Easter). Both religious observations were adopted after the Ancient Egyptian Easter [see the last chapter of this book for details].

9.2 THE BIBLICAL JESUS

1. How Did He Die?

There appear to be conflicting accounts of how Jesus died.

– The New Testament claims that Jesus was crucified:

- *And they crucified him ...* [Matthew, 27:35]

- *And when they had crucified him ...* [Mark, 15:24]

- *And when they were come to the place, which is called Calvary, there they crucified him ...* [Luke, 23:33]

- *Then the soldiers, when they had crucified Jesus ...* [John, 19:23]

- *Paul stated*:
  ... Jesus, whom ye have crucified ... [Acts, 2:36]

However, crucifixion was a Roman, not an Israelite form of execution. This form of execution would be expected had Jesus been tried and condemned by a Roman court, which was never the case. He was sentenced to death by the Jewish hierarchy. The Israelites <u>hanged the condemned person from a tree</u>, as per [Deuteronomy, 21:22]:

> **<u>And if a man have committed a sin worthy of death ... thou hang him on a tree</u>**

<u>-There are also references in the New Testament to Jesus being hanged</u>, as per the following accounts by Peter:

- *... Jesus, whom ye slew and hanged on a tree* [Acts, 5:30]

- *And we are witnesses to all that he did both in the country of the Jews and in Jerusalem. They put him to death by hanging him on a tree ...* [Acts, 10:39]

- *... they took him down from the tree, and laid him in a tomb* [Acts, 13:29]

– The Old Testament states that Jesus was hanged from a tree:

> **His body shall not remain all night upon the tree, but thou shalt in any wise bury him that day; (for he that is hanged is accursed of God) ...** [Deuteronomy, 21:23]

– The Talmud refers to Jesus as having been

a. <u>crucified</u> (as per T. Sanh., 9.7):

It seems that the king [Jesus] is crucified

b. and <u>hanged</u>:

Jesus was hanged **[b. Sanh., 106b]** *They hanged him on the eve of the Passover* **[b. Sanh., 43a]**

=> The cross is mentioned in the Gospel of Thomas as a symbol not of death but eternal spiritual life in the same sense that we find in both the canonical gospels [Mark 8:34, and Paul's Letter to the Galatians 2:20].

Paul's theology of the Cross did not focus on the suffering and death of Jesus, but on his resurrection and the promise of eternal life.

Likewise in Ancient Egypt, the ankh, a cross with a circle or loop at the top, was widely used in Ancient Egyptian culture as a sign of eternal life. It was frequently placed in the hands of the dead as *"an emblem both of incarnation and of new life to come."* Additionally, the sign of the cross was commonly formed by the arms of the deceased as were always found on the breasts of mummies.

=> As a result, *hanging* was the mode of execution and *crucifixion* was/is a figure of speech indicative of eternal life.

2. Who Condemned Him? And Why?

The New Testament clearly and totally blames the Israelite priests for condemning him to death. He was at variance with the

Jewish hierarchy. Their charge against him was blasphemy of the Jewish Scriptures. The Bible did not indicate any charge against him by the Romans whatsoever. Examples are:

a. *"The Jews answered him, 'We have a law, and by that law he ought to die, because he has made himself the Son of God."* [John, 19:7]

Son of God was the title of all Egyptian kings since time immemorial.

b. Paul said, in I Thessalonians, 2:14-15: *the Jews, who killed the Lord Jesus*

c. *"When morning came, all the chief priests and the elders took counsel against Jesus to put him to death;"* [Matthew, 27:1]

d. *"Pilate then called together the chief priests and the rulers of the people, and said to them, 'You brought me this man as one who was perverting the people; and after examining him before you, behold, I did not find this man guilty of any of your charges against him; neither did Herod, for he sent him back to us. Behold, nothing deserving death has been done by him; I will therefore chastise him and release him."* [Luke, 23:13-16]

e. *"He (Pilate) went out to the Jews again, and told them, 'I find no crime in him."* [John, 18:38]

f. *"Pilate went out again, and said to them, 'Behold, I am bringing him out to you, that you may know that I find no crime in him."* [John, 19:4]

3. Who Killed Him?

The New Testament identifies the Jews as the killers, e.g. [I Thessalonians, 2:14-15]

... The Jews, who killed both the Lord Jesus and the prophets, and drove us out, and displease God and oppose all men ...

=> The Talmud clearly identifies Jesus' killer as Pinhas, the Israelite priest who lived in the 14th century BCE and was a companion of Moses. The rabbis accepted that the Israelite priests were responsible for the condemnation of Jesus as a punishment for his having led Israel astray.

... they hanged Jesus (the Nazarene) ... because he hath practiced magic and deceived and led astray Israel [b. Sanh., 43a]

The Talmud is quite specific: *"Pinhas ... killed him* [Jesus]" [b. Sanh., 106b].

Pinhas (Phinehas, to use the name shown in the Old Testament) was the priest, the son of Eleazar, the son of Aaron, who is identified in the Book of Numbers as a contemporary of Moses.

Phinehas looked upon Jesus' teachings of religious co-existence as blasphemy. On the eve of the Passover, Pinhas/Phinehas killed Jesus in the Tabernacle at the foot of Mount Sinai.

PART III : THE EGYPTIAN CHRISTIAN ESSENCE

CHAPTER 10 : THE EGYPTIAN ROOTS OF CHRISTIANITY

10.1 THE EGYPTIAN ROOTS OF CHRISTIANITY

The very thing that is now called the Christian religion was already in existence in Ancient Egypt long before the adoption of the New Testament.

The British Egyptologist, E.A. Wallis Budge, in his book *Egyptian Religion: Egyptian Ideas of Future Life* (1975), writes:

> *... the Egyptians possessed, some six thousand years ago, a religion and a system of morality which, when stripped of all corrupt accretions, stand second to none among those which have been developed by the greatest nations of the world.* [pg xii]

Long ago, the Ancient Egyptians believed in the coming of a messiah, a Madonna and her child, a virgin birth, and the incarnation of the spirit in flesh. The Ancient Egyptian texts reveal irrefutable proof that **the entire body of Christian doctrine is simply a revamped and mutilated Egyptianism**. The early Christian church accepted these ancient truths as the very tenets of Christianity, but disavowed their origins. Plagiarizing the Egyptian religion was noted by several brave writers. The British Egyptologist, Sir E. A. Wallis Budge, wrote in his book, *The Gods of the Egyptians* [1969]:

> *The new religion (Christianity) which was preached there by*

St. Mark and his immediate followers, in all essentials so closely resembled that which was the outcome of the worship of Osiris, Isis, and Horus.

The similarities, noted by Budge and everyone who has compared the Egyptian Osiris/Isis/ Horus allegory to the Gospel story, are powerful. Both accounts are practically the same: e.g. the supernatural conception, the divine birth, the struggles against the enemy in the wilderness, and the resurrection from the dead to eternal life. The main difference between them is that the Gospel tale is considered historical and the Osiris/Isis/ Horus cycle is an allegory. The spiritual message of the Osiris/ Isis/ Horus allegory and the Christian revelation are exactly the same.

Gerald Massey, after studying the similarities between the Osiris/Isis/Horus allegory [shown in the next chapter] and the Gospel story, concluded in his book *Ancient Egypt* (1970) that the Christian revelation is Egyptian in source. He believed that early Christians in their 'ignorance' (his word) took the Egyptian spiritual teaching and turned it into a spiritual and historical event. Gerald Massey has traced nearly 200 instances of immediate correspondence between the allegorical Egyptian material and the allegedly historical Christian writings about Jesus.

Christianity began as a cult with almost wholly Egyptian origins and motivations in the 1st century, and by the 4th century it had utterly turned its back on its Egyptian origin. The Church of the 3rd and 4th centuries first tried to ridicule the whole suggestion of plagiarism. When that failed, they took the bizarre tack that the devil had planted these similarities in the Egyptian religions centuries before, in order to deceive potential converts. When that didn't work either, they became extremely violent, which led to murder, destruction, and terrorizing the masses.

10.2 ALLEGORY AND FICTIONAL HISTORY

The cosmological knowledge of Ancient Egypt was expressed in story form, which is a superior means for expressing both physical and metaphysical concepts. Well crafted allegories are the only way to explain the deepest truths about God, creation, life, the soul, our place in the universe, and our struggle to evolve to higher levels of insight and understanding.

Any good writer or lecturer knows that stories are better than exposition for explaining the behavior of things, because the relationships of parts to each other, and to the whole, are better maintained by the mind. The Egyptian sages transformed common factual nouns and adjectives (indicators of qualities) into proper but conceptual nouns. These were, in addition, personified so that they could be woven into narratives. Storytellers were specially qualified people, for *"the word is mightier than the sword"*.

Allegories are intentionally chosen as a means of communicating knowledge. Allegories dramatize cosmic laws, principles, processes, and relationships and functions, and express them in a way that's easy to understand. Once the inner meanings of the allegories have been revealed, they become marvels of simultaneous scientific and philosophical completeness and conciseness. The more they are studied, the richer they become. The 'inner dimension' of the teachings embedded into each story make them capable of revealing several layers of knowledge, according to the stage of development of the listener. The "secrets" are revealed as one evolves higher. The higher we get, the more we see. It is always there.

The Egyptians did not believe their allegories were historical facts. They believed *IN* them: in the sense that they believed in the truth beneath the stories.

The Ancient Egyptians had numerous allegories that were

adopted in the Bible as historical events, such as the Autobiography of Sinuhe, which was adopted in the Bible as David and Goliath, as well as the Osiris/Isis/Horus allegory [see the next chapter]. The biblical stories have completely mutilated the Ancient Egyptian allegories.

The Christian religion threw away and lost the very soul of their meaning when it mistranslated the Ancient Egyptian allegorical language into alleged history instead of viewing it as a spiritual allegory. The result was a pathetic, blind faith in a kind of emotional and superstitious super-naturalism, and effectively aborted the real power of the story/allegory to transform the life of every individual.

CHAPTER 11 : THE ANCIENT EGYPTIAN/ CHRISTIAN HOLY FAMILIES

The Egyptian allegory of Isis and Osiris explains practically all facets of life. This love story resonates with betrayal and loyalty, death and rebirth, forgetting and remembering, evil and righteousness, duty and compassion, the manifestation of the forces of nature, the meaning of sisterhood and brotherhood and of motherhood/fatherhood/son-hood, and the mysteries of the body, the soul, and the spirit.

The following is a shortened version of the Isis and Osiris Egyptian allegory, provided so as to highlight the Egyptian source of Christianity. This narrative is compiled from Ancient Egyptian temples, tombs, and papyri, dated 3,000 years before Christianity, and goes as follows:

> The self-created Atum begat the twins Shu and Tef-nut, who in turn gave birth to Nut (the sky/spirit) and Geb (the earth/

matter). [More details about the creation of the universe and man are in a later chapter.]

The union of Nut (spirit) and Geb (matter) produced four offspring: Osiris, Isis, Seth, and Nepthys.

Like the biblical Jesus, Osiris symbolizes the divine in a mortal form combining both spirit (**Nut**) and matter (**Geb**).

According to the Ancient Egyptian traditions, Osiris came to earth for the benefit of mankind, bearing the title of *Manifester of Good and Truth* – likewise, the biblical Jesus.

The Egyptian allegory goes that Osiris married Isis, and Seth married Nephthys. Osiris became King of the land (Egypt) after marrying Isis.

Osiris brought civilization and spirituality to the people, enabling them thus, to achieve prosperity. He gave them a body of laws to regulate their conduct, settled their disputes justly, and instructed them in the science of spiritual development.

Having civilized Egypt, he traveled around the world to spread the same instructions. Wherever Osiris went he brought peace and learning to the people:

> **Between the two evangelists (Osiris and Jesus), there are vivid similarities. The divine son comes down from heaven. God came down to earth to guide the world. Both had traveled to spread the word.**

Osiris induced people to accept his teachings not by force of arms, but by the use of persuasive lectures, spiritual hymns, and music. Diodorus of Sicily wrote, in *Book I* [18, 4]:

> ***Osiris was laughter-loving and fond of music and the dance;* Similarly, the biblical Jesus was persuasive and was**

celebrated as *Lord of the Dance* in a Christmas carol from the Middle Ages.

When Osiris returned from his mission, he was greeted with a royal feast where he was tricked by Seth—the evil one—and his accomplices into lying down inside a makeshift coffin. The evil group quickly closed and sealed the chest and threw it into the Nile. Seth became the new Pharaoh as the coffin containing the lifeless body of Osris flowed into the Mediterranean Sea.

Both Jesus and Osiris were betrayed by dinner guests (Jesus by Judas, and Osiris by Seth at their own privately-held banquets. The biblical Jesus' age was assumed to be 23 years old and Osiris was 28 years old—both were young.

Meanwhile, Isis, upon receiving the news of Osiris' fate and disappearance, was in grief and vowed never to rest until she found the *Manifester of Truth*—Osiris.

Isis searched everywhere, accosting everyone she met, including children: for it was said that children had/have the power of divination.

Children, with the power of divination, are acknowledged by the biblical Jesus in the New Testament.

The story goes that one day during her search, Isis requested shelter at the house of a poor woman.

This point signifies the paramount feature of the Egyptian teachings where one was/is taught not to consider oneself to be superior to others, but to rank oneself as the poorest, lowest, and most humble of mankind. This applies to everyone—including Isis, the Queen.

By fabricating humble roots for Jesus and his family,

Christiandom missed the point that it is the powerful who must learn to be humble.

Humility is symbolized in the action of the Christ King mounting an ass: that represents the ego and false pride. This is truly Ancient Egyptian symbolism.

The story continues that the coffin of Osiris was swept by the waves to the shoreline of a foreign land. A tree sprang up and grew around it, enclosing the body of Osiris in its trunk. The tree grew large, beautiful, and fragrant. [See the Ancient Egyptian temple depiction below.] News of this magnificent tree came to the king of this alien land, who ordered that the tree be cut down and its trunk brought to him. He utilized the trunk as a pillar in his house without knowing the great secret it contained within.

This is a reference to the Tree of Life, and with all that this implies. It is also a reference to the Tet (Djed) pillar of Osiris.

In Christianity, this became the Christmas tree.

Isis had a revelation in her dreams that Osiris' body was in this alien land, so she immediately traveled there. When she arrived she dressed as a commoner and befriended the queen's handmaidens and was able to get a job in the palace as a nurse of the baby prince.

Isis, the Queen of Egypt, practiced the Egyptian teachings that emphasize the practice of humility by serving others without exception to achieve union with her love—The Divine.

Later on, Isis confessed her identity to the queen, as well as the purpose of her mission. Isis then asked the king that the pillar be given to her. The king granted her request, and she cut deep into the trunk and took out the chest.

Isis returned back to Egypt with the chest containing Osiris' lifeless body. She hid the body in the marshes of the Nile Delta. Isis used her magical powers [according to *Pyramid Texts* number 632, 1636, and murals at Abydos and Philae] to transform herself into a dove. Drawing Osiris' essence from him, she conceived a child—Horus. In other words, Isis was impregnated by the holy ghost of Osiris. [See the Ancient Egyptian temple depiction below.]

>>This action symbolizes reincarnation and spiritual rebirth—a key to understanding the Egyptian belief in life after death.

Shown above is an Ancient Egyptian temple depiction showing Isis on the left, as her magical essence embodied in the flying dove draws the essence of Osiris to be impregnated. On the left, a frog-headed netert (goddess), Heqet, symbolizes the power of fertility, representing conception and procreation.

>Isis' conception of Horus by no living man is the oldest doc-umented version of immaculate conception. The *supernatural conception* and the *virgin birth* of Horus found their way into Christianity.

Isis' role in the Egyptian Model Story and the story of the Virgin Mary are strikingly similar: for both were able to conceive without male impregnation, and, as such, Isis was revered as the *Virgin Mother*.

– More about the Ancient Egyptian concept of holy (virgin) conception/birth is found earlier in this book.

– More about the ideal of virginity in the Ancient Egyptian culture is found earlier in this book.

When Seth heard about the new child (Horus), Seth went to kill the newborn. Hearing that Seth was coming, **Isis was told to take him to a secluded spot in the marshes of the Nile Delta** [as per the Ancient Egyptian temple depiction shown herein].

This is the source of the story in which Herod, upon hearing about the birth of the biblical Jesus, set out to destroy all the newborn males. In the New Testament the angel of the Lord says to Joseph: "Arise and take the young child and his mother and flee into Egypt."

Like Isis, the Virgin Mary is celebrated as the "Queen of Marshes".

An Ancient Egyptian festival celebrating the birth of Horus, was held on 25 December, and it resembles the Christian festival of Christmas. The celebration was called *The Day of the Child in His Cradle*, and was held at the court and the chapel of the Dendera Temple. [More information in a later chapter.]

The story continues that one night (while Isis was giving birth to Horus in hiding), when the moon was full, the evil Seth and his accomplices found the chest containing the dead body of Osiris and cut him into 14 pieces (the number 14 symbolizes the number of days required to shape a full moon). Osiris represents the lunar principle in the universe and is known as Osiris *the Moon*.

When Isis heard about how Seth and his accomplices cut Osiris into different pieces and scattered them throughout the land, her job was to search near and far, to collect and put the broken pieces back together.

1. *To bind or tie together* is the meaning of the "Latin" word *religio*, which is the root of the word 'religion'.

2. By remembering and recollecting the story of Isis and Osiris, we keep in our hearts a tale that expresses, in Joseph Campbell's words, *"the immanence of divinity in the phenomenal forms of the universe."*

As soon as Horus had grown to manhood, he challenged Seth for the right to the throne in what was called the "Great Quarrel/ Struggle in the Wilderness."

Isis, with the help of others, collected all the pieces... all except for the phallus (indicative of physical reproduction), which had been swallowed by a fish in the Nile. She then reunited the dismembered body of Osiris and, with the help of others, wrapped it in linen bandages and mummified it.

Thoth, Isis, and Horus performed the *Ceremony of Opening The Mouth* upon the mummy, and Osiris was brought back to life as the Judge and King of the Dead (the past), while Horus was to take his place as king of the living (the present). Seth remained the *Lord of Wilderness*.

This represents the everlasting perpetual cycle of the spiritual power on earth: *The King is dead: (Osiris); Long live the King (Horus).*

As the Perfect Shepherd, Osiris is usually shown in a mummified, bearded human body, carrying the shepherd's crook (being the shepherd of mankind) and the flail (symbolizing the ability to separate wheat from chaff).

The shepherd motif is encountered in the 23rd Psalm; *"thy rod and thy staff, they comfort me"*.

In many ways, the account of the Resurrection of Jesus is similar to that of Osiris. Like Osiris, he is said to have risen from the dead. The Ancient Egyptians believed, as did the early Christians (Hebrews, 4:14), that *"man cannot be saved"* by a distant Almighty, but only by one who has shared the experience of human suffering and death.

– Both Osiris and Jesus suffered and died.

– Both Osiris and Jesus were shortly resurrected after their deaths. Reassuming earthly form, they demonstratively affirmed proper conduct and its other-worldly rewards, after which time they returned to heaven, having "saved the world".

– Both became the savior to whom men and women turned for assurance of immortality.

The medieval Passion plays concerning the death and resurrection of Jesus closely parallels the death and resurrection of the Egyptian King as Osiris.

Finally, the biblical story about the raising from the dead of *El-Asar* or *Lazarus* has maintained the Ancient Egyptian name/concept of Osiris whose name in the Ancient Egyptian tongue was *'Asar'*. The miracle described in John's Gospel was never an historic event. Instead it was a recurring, deeply archetypal and widely used symbol of God's power to resurrect the dead.

CHAPTER 12 : THE WAY OF HORUS/CHRIST

12.1 LIKE FATHER LIKE SON

In Bible teachings, Christ is sometimes referred to as the "Son of God" and at other times simply as God. In John's Gospel, Christ says, *"I and the Father are one."*

The history of the political and doctrinal struggles within the Church during and after the 4th century has largely been written in terms of the disputes over the nature of God and Christ and the relationship between them. All the "apparent" conflicting theories about these natures can be explained in the Ancient Egyptian context of the relationship between Osiris—the Father—and his Divine Son—namely Horus.

The interchangeable relationship between the Father and the Son is eloquently illustrated in several places in Egypt [as shown below], whereby Horus is being born out of Osiris, with the sun disk rising with the newborn.

The Egyptians believed in the anthropomorphic divinity, or Horus (Christ) ideal, whose life in this world and the world beyond was typical of the ideal life of man. The chief embodiment of this divinity was Osiris and his son, Horus. Neither, however, was ever regarded as historical, but were allegorical.

Osiris represents the mortal man carrying within himself the capacity and power of spiritual salvation. Every Egyptian's hope was/is resurrection in a transformed body and immortality, which could only be realized through the death and resurrection of Osiris within each person.

Osiris symbolizes the subconscious—the capacity to act, to do; whereas Horus symbolizes consciousness, will, and the potential to act; to do.

12.2 THE AWAKENING POTENTIALS

In the Egyptian model story [in the previous chapter], Osiris wasn't actually dead at first—he was in a coma; a state of complete unawareness where people think they're awake and aware, but they aren't. To bring about the Hope [Horus] and to make him manifest, people have to resurrect Osiris to bring him out of the coma. This is how our souls and spirits and life essence are able to pass from this world into the more evolved states of creation towards divine union.

The British Egyptologist, Sir E.A. Wallis Budge, summed it up on page vii of his book, *Osiris and the Egyptian Resurrection, Vol. I*, as follows:

> *The central figure of the ancient Egyptian religion was Osiris, and the chief fundamentals of his cult were the belief in his divinity, death, resurrection, and absolute control of the destinies of the bodies and souls of men. The central point of each Osirian's religion was his hope of resurrection in a transformed body and of immortality, which could only be realized by him through the death and resurrection of Osiris.*

All dead persons were/are equated to Osiris, because Osiris is a cosmic principle and not a historical person. The Egyptian religion was an inclusive religion where Osiris lives within each of us, which facilitated a true understanding of who we are and who we are intended to become.

The principle that makes life come from apparent death was/is called Osiris, who symbolizes the power of renewal. Osiris represents the process, growth, and the underlying cyclical aspects of the universe.

From the earliest period of Ancient Egyptian history, the Egyptians believed that Osiris was of divine origin partly divine and partly human, who had raised himself from the dead without having seen corruption. What Osiris had effected for himself, he could effect for man. As a model, the Ancient Egyptians believed that what Osiris did, they could do. Because he had conquered death, the righteous too might conquer death and attain everlasting life. They would rise again and attain everlasting life.

Shown below is one of the numerous illustrations showing the Resurrection Principle — Osiris. On the left, the bearded neter (god) presents "life" (the ankh) to him and voicing words of power.

The theme in the *Egyptian Book of the Caverns* talks about the necessity for death and dissolution (of the carnal and material) prior to the birth of the spiritual.

This is echoed by the biblical Jesus when he says:

> **Except a corn of wheat fall into the ground and die, it abideth alone: but if it die, it bringeth forth much fruit [John 12:24]**

Paul also refers to the same principle in I Corinthians 15:36:

> **... that which thou sowest is not quickened, except it die.**

Another example is the biblical wine symbolism, which can be traced to Ancient Egypt where the walls of the Ancient Egyptian tombs show vintners pressing new wine [as per the above Ancient Egyptian tomb scene], and wine-making is everywhere a constant metaphor of spiritual processes and the themes of transformation and inner power.

In places in the Egyptian scripts, Osiris himself was characterized as the vine.

The soul, or the portion of *god* within, causes the divine ferment in the body of life. It's developed there, as on the vine, by the sun of man's spiritual self. The fermented potency of wine was, at its deepest spiritual level, a symbol of the presence of the incarnated God within the spiritually aware person.

12.3 THE WAY OF HORUS/CHRIST

Horus declares, in *The Egyptian Book of Coming Forth by Light* (incorrectly known as *The Egyptian Book of the Dead*) [c. 78]: *"I am Horus in glory"; "I am the Lord of Light"; "I am the victorious one . . . I am the heir of endless time"; "I am he that knoweth the paths of heaven."*

The above Ancient Egyptian verses were echoed later in Jesus' words *"I am the light of the world"* and again, *"I am the way, the truth and the life."*

Horus, in the Ancient Egyptian language, means *He who is above*. As such, Horus represents the realized divine principle. Horus is the personification of the goal of all initiated teachings, and is always depicted as accompanying the realized soul to the Source.

In the Ancient Egyptian allegory, Horus brought Osiris to life. On Judgment Day, Horus shows the Way to Osiris. He acts as a mediator between the deceased and Osiris, The Father. All Egyptians wanted/want Horus to bring them (when dead) to life.

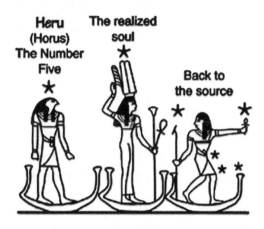

Likewise in Christianity, the Christian motif was/is based on the need for a mediator and a son of god as an all-powerful shepherd and a begotten savior living among the common man.

As the model of earthly existence, Horus is represented in several forms and aspects to correspond with the stages of the process of spiritualization.

12.4 PROGRESSIVE SOWING AND REAPING

According to the Ancient Egyptian teachings, though all creation is spiritual in origin, man is born mortal and contains within himself the seed of the divine. His purpose in this life is to nourish that seed, and his reward, if successful, is eternal life, where he will reunite with his divine origin.

The typical Ancient Egyptian sowing and reaping tomb scene is symbolically similar to the biblical parable:

Whatsoever a man soweth, that shall he also reap.

This was intended to be a spiritual message, not agricultural advice.

Man comes into the world with higher divine faculties, which are the essence of his/her salvation, in an unawakened state. The way of the Egyptian teachings is, therefore, a system of practices aimed at awakening man's dormant higher faculties.

The awakening emphasis of the Egyptian teachings cannot be overstressed. Moral behavior, for example, does not come about from merely learning certain values, but is gained by both the mind and acquired experience. Inner purification must be completed by practicing good social behavior in ordinary daily life. Every action impresses itself upon the heart. The inward being of a person is really the reflection of his deeds and actions. Doing good deeds thus establishes good inner qualities, and the virtues impressed upon the heart in turn govern the actions of the limbs. As each act, thought, and deed makes an image on the heart, it becomes an attribute of the person. This maturation of the soul through acquired attributes leads to progressive mystical visions and an ultimate unification with the Divine.

The Ancient Egyptian wisdom has always laid great emphasis on the cultivation of ethical behavior and service to society.

In Ancient Egypt, the concept of **Ma-at** has permeated all Egyptian writings from the earliest times and throughout Egyptian history. **Ma-at**, The Way, encompasses the virtues, goals, and duties that define acceptable, if not ideal, social interaction and personal behavior.

A summary of the Egyptian concept of righteousness can be found in what is popularly known as the *Negative Confessions* [as discussed later in this chapter]. A more detailed picture of a righteous man and the expected conduct and the ideas of responsibility and retribution can be obtained from the walls of tomb-chapels and in several literary compositions that are usually defined as wisdom texts of systematic instructions, composed of maxims and precepts. Among them are the 30 chapters of the *Teaching of Amenemope* (Amenhotep III), which contain many wisdom texts that were later adopted in the Old Testament's *Book of Proverbs*.

Numerous verbal parallels occur between this Egyptian text and the Bible, such as the opening lines of the first chapter:

> **Give your ears, listen to the words that are spoken, give your mind to interpreting them. It is profitable to put them in your heart.**

The progression along the spiritual Path is acquired through striving, and is a matter of conscious disciplined action. Each new/raised consciousness is equivalent to a new awakening. The levels of consciousness are referred to as *death—rebirth*. Such thinking has pervaded Ancient (and present-day) Egypt, where *birth* and *rebirth* are a constant theme. The word *death* is employed in a figurative sense. The theme that man must *"die before he dies"* or that he must be *"born again"* in his present life is taken symbolically, or is commemorated by a ritual. In this, the candidate has to pass through certain specific experiences (technically termed *"deaths"*). A good example is baptism, which was the main objective at Easter, after Lent, representing death of the old self by immersing into water and the rising of the new/renewed self by coming out of the water.

12.5 JUDGMENT DAY

In a book of instructions, an Egyptian King advised his son, the prince, to attain the highest qualities because upon his death, he would see his whole lifetime in a single instant, and his performance on earth would be reviewed and evaluated by the judges. Even as far back as the period of the 6th Dynasty [4,300 years ago], we find the idea that <u>heaven was reserved for those who had performed their duty to man and to the Divine Powers while on earth. No exceptions were made for a King or anyone else.</u>

As stated earlier, Ancient Egyptians expressed their metaphysical beliefs in a story form, like a sacred drama or a *mystery play*. The following are the Egyptians' symbolic representations of the process of the Judgment Day *Mystery Play*.

1. The soul of the deceased is led to the Hall of Judgment of the Double-**Ma-at**. She is *double* because the scale balances only when there is an equality of opposing forces. **Ma-at's** symbol is the ostrich feather, representing judgment or truth. Her feather is customarily mounted on the scales.

2. Anubis, as opener of the way, guides the deceased to the scales and weighs the heart.

The heart, as a metaphor for conscience, is weighed against the feather of truth, to determine the fate of the deceased.

[1. Ma-at, 2. Anubis, 3. Amam (Ammit), 4. Thoth, 5. The deceased, 6. Horus, 7. Osiris, 8. 42 Judges/Assessors]

3. The seated Grand Ancestor—Osiris—presides in the Hall of Justice. The jury consists of 42 judges/assessors. Each judge has a specific jurisdiction over a specific sin or fault.

4. The spirit of the deceased denies committing each sin/fault before its assigned judge by reciting the *42 Negative Confessions*. These Negative Confessions come from *Chapter CXXV of The Book of the Coming Forth by Light* (incorrectly known as *The Book of the Dead*).

The assigned juror/judge will declare his/her acceptance by declaring **Maa-Kheru** (*True of Voice/Action*).

Here is a translation of the *42 Negative Confessions*. Some of them may seem repetitive, but this is caused by the inability to translate the exact intent and meaning of the original language.

1. I have not done iniquity.
2. I have not robbed with violence.
3. I have not stolen.
4. I have done no murder; I have done no harm.
5. I have not defrauded offerings.

6. I have not diminished obligations.

7. I have not plundered the neteru.

8. I have not spoken lies.

9. I have not uttered evil words.

10. I have not caused pain.

11. I have not committed fornication.

12. I have not caused shedding of tears.

13. I have not dealt deceitfully.

14. I have not transgressed.

15. I have not acted guilefully.

16. I have not laid waste the ploughed land.

17. I have not been an eavesdropper.

18. I have not set my lips in motion (against any man).

19. I have not been angry and wrathful except for a just cause.

20. I have not defiled the wife of any man.

21. I have not been a man of anger.

22. I have not polluted myself.

23. I have not caused terror.

24. I have not burned with rage.

25. I have not stopped my ears against the words of Right and Truth. (Ma-at)

26. I have not worked grief.

27. I have not acted with insolence.

28. I have not stirred up strife.

29. I have not judged hastily.

30. I have not sought for distinctions.

31. I have not multiplied words exceedingly.

32. I have not done neither harm nor ill.

33. I have not cursed the King (i.e. violation of laws)

34. I have not fouled the water.

35. I have not spoken scornfully.

36. I have never cursed the neteru.

37. I have not stolen.

38. I have not defrauded the offerings of the neteru.

39. I have not plundered the offerings of the blessed dead.

40. I have not filched the food of the infant.

41. I have not sinned against the neter of my native town.

42. I have not slaughtered with evil intent the cattle of the neter.

5. Thoth, scribe of the neteru (gods, goddesses), records the verdict as Anubis weighs the heart against the feather of truth. The outcome is either:

a. If the pans are not balanced, the unperfected soul will be reborn again (reincarnated) in a new physical vehicle (body) in order to provide the soul an opportunity for further development on earth. This cycle of life/death/renewal continues until the soul is perfected by fulfilling the *42 Negative Confessions* during his life on earth.

b. If the two pans are perfectly balanced, Osiris gives favorable judgment, and the perfected soul will go through the process of transformation and the subsequent rebirth.

Ancient Egyptian transformational (funerary) texts show that the resurrected pure soul, justified and regenerated, attains a place in the retinue of the **neteru** (gods, goddesses)—the cosmic forces—and eventually takes part in the unceasing round of activity that permits a continued existence of the universe. The role of the successful soul is described in the Ancient Egyptian writing:

... becomes a star of gold and joins the company of Re, and sails with him across the sky in his boat of millions of years.

12.6 THE GLORY

In the Ancient Egyptian texts, the realized soul achieves glory and joins the Divine Origin. Likewise, the Bible tells us that Jesus is said to have achieved glory only after his death and Resurrection:

> ... *God, that raised him up from the dead and gave him glory ...*
> **[I Peter, 1:21]**

Glory is the radiant beauty of splendor and magnificence—heaven or the bliss of heaven—which is attained by the highest achievement. Glory is represented in artwork as a halo or a circle of light. In Ancient Egypt, the neter (god) Re represents the Light and is depicted as a circle.

The relationship between the cycle of death and resurrection is reflected in the Egyptian form of the "name"of Osiris being **Ausar**, which consists of two syllables—**Aus-Ra**. The first syllable of the name (Aus-Ra) is pronounced *Aus* or *Os*, meaning "strength, might, power". The name of the **neter** (god) means something like the *strength of Re*. This meaning describes the true essence of the neter (god) Osiris.

In the cycle of **Aus-Ra**, **Ausar** (Osiris) is identified with the moon, the light of the night regions of the dead. **Ausar's** Light is a reflection of **Ra** (Re), in one of his manifestations as the sun.

Ausar died (analogous to the moon's departure, near the end of the lunar month) and was resurrected the third day after that. The third day is the beginning of a new moon, i.e. a renewed **Ausar**. This is reminiscent of the Easter celebration where, like **Ausar**, the biblical Jesus died on Friday and was resurrected the third day (Sunday) as a new life.

Ausar (Osiris) is written in hieroglyphs with the glyph of the throne and the eye, combining the concepts of legitimacy and divinity.

Ra (Re) is associated with the glyph of the eye. The most distinctive Egyptian symbol is the eye, which plays many complex and subtle roles. The eye is the part of the body able to perceive the light, and is therefore a symbol for spiritual ability.

Ra (Re) is the cosmic principle of energy that moves toward death, and **Ausar** (Osiris) represents the process of rebirth. Thus, the terms of life and death become interchangeable: life means slow dying; death means resurrection to new life. The dead person in death is identified with **Ausar**, but he will come to life agai, and will be identified with **Ra**.

CHAPTER 13 : GENESIS: THE MUTILATED ANCIENT EGYPTIAN COSMOLOGY

13.1 THE ORDERLY CREATION PROCESS

For the deeply religious people of Egypt, the creation of the universe was not a physical event (Big Bang) that just happened. It was an orderly event that was pre-planned and executed according to an orderly Divine Law that governs the physical and metaphysical worlds. So, we read in the *Book of Knowing the Creations of Ra and Overcoming Apep* (Apophis), known as the *Bremner-Rhind Papyrus*:

> *I conceived the Divine Plan of Law or Order (Maa) to make all forms. I was alone.*

Creation is the sorting out (giving definition to/bringing order to) of all the chaos (the undifferentiated energy/matter and consciousness) of the primeval state. All of the Ancient Egyptian accounts of creation exhibited this with well-defined, clearly demarcated stages.

All Ancient Egyptian creation texts begin with The Self-Begotten and Self-Existent, who lived alone in a primeval watery mass. Then God planned the creation of the universe in an orderly fashion. God then uttered words of power that began the process of creation. It should be noted that the Ancient Egyptian creation process is complete, logical, orderly, and conforms with later scientific findings in the Western world. On the other hand, the same accounts of creation in the Bible are basically mutilated disorderly copies of Ancient Egyptian cosmology, as shown below.

13.2 IN THE BEGINNING

Genesis 1:3-5 describes the pre-creation state of the world:

The earth was without form and void; and darkness was upon the face of the deep; and the spirit (or wind/air) of God was moving over the face of the waters.

Likewise, in Ancient Egypt, every Egyptian creation text begins with the same basic belief that before the beginning of things, there was a liquidy *primeval abyss* everywhere; dark, endless, and without boundaries or directions. Egyptians called this cosmic ocean/watery chaos **Nu/Ny/Nun**—the unpolarized state of matter. The Bible, however, chose the term "Earth", which is a cause of major confusion.

The Ancient Egyptian description of the pre-creation state of the universe was agreed to, in recent times, by Western scientists. Their clue came when they noticed that the galaxies are all moving away from us, and that a galaxy that is five times farther away than another is going five times as fast; ten times farther, ten times as fast, and so on. This led to the conclusion that there must have been a time in the past when all the matter of the universe was packed tightly together, to an infinite density. This matter is described by scientists as a very stiff *neutron soup*, where there were neither electrons nor protons; only neutrons forming one huge, extremely dense nucleus.

In addition to the chaotic pre-creation state, biblical text [*and the spirit (or wind/air) of God was moving over the face of the waters*] shows the presence of God independent of the chaotic pre-creation state of the universe.

In the Egyptian papyrus known as the *Leyden Papyrus*, the **neter** (god) **Amen/Amon/Amun** (which means *hidden*) represents the hidden or occult force underlying creation. He is the *Breath of Life*. Even though he is indefinable himself, he is the reason why the universe can be defined.

The Bible repeats the Ancient Egyptian representation of **Amen**, in Revelations 3:14:

> **And to the angel of the church in La-o-di-ce-a write: The words of the Amen, the faithful and true witness, the beginning of God's creation.**

It must be noted that **Amen** (in Ancient Egypt) is not an entity, but one of the multitude of attributes of the One Supreme Being. As noted earlier, the Ancient Egyptians believed in One God who was self-produced, self-existent, immortal, invisible, eternal, omniscient, almighty, etc. This One God was represented through the functions and attributes of "His" domain. These attributes were called the **neteru** (pronounced *net-er-u*; masculine singular: **neter**; feminine singular: **netert**). In other words, the ALL (**neteru**) are the One. The Ancient Egyptians utilized pictorial symbols to represent the divine attributes and actions which correspond to our common saying *"a picture is worth a thousand words"*. In other words, the Ancient Egyptian pictorial symbols were not intended to be looked upon as real personages.

13.3 THE WORD

The first action of creation—namely the Divine Utterance of the creation—is found in St. John's Gospel, which begins:

> **In the beginning was the Word, and the Word was with God, and the Word was God.**

Thousands of years earlier, the Egyptian *Book of the Coming Forth by Day* (incorrectly known as the *Book of the Dead*), the oldest written text in the world, contains a strikingly parallel passage:

I am the Eternal, I am Ra (Re)... I am that which created the Word ... I am the Word ...

The Egyptian texts state that the created universe came out of the mouth (of **Ra**), and the mouth is the symbol of Unity— the One—in hieroglyphs. The creation process, i.e. transformation (differentiation), is achieved through sound (the Word) as the prime mover of the inert energy of the chaotic state of the pre-creation matter.

The *Word* (sound variations) *is mightier than the sword* has been accepted by modern science, which recognizes that there are various types of sound waves. We know that infra sound waves can't be detected by our ears, but they can shake buildings and destroy body organs. Also, the ultrasound waves cannot be detected by our ears, but doctors use this power as a kind of knifeless scalpel in microsurgery. We also know that a soprano singer can shatter glass with her voice.

Egyptian creation texts repeatedly stress the belief of creation by the Word. We find that in the *Book of the Divine Cow* (found in the shrines of Twt-Ankh-Amen), **Ra** (Re) creates the heavens and its hosts merely by pronouncing some words whose sound alone evokes the names of things—and these things then appear at his bidding. As its name is pronounced, so the thing comes into being, for the name is a reality; the thing itself.

The *word* (any word) is, scientifically, a vibrational complex element which is a wave phenomenon characterized by movements of variable frequency and intensity. Each sound-wave frequency has its own geometrical corresponding form. Modern science has confirmed a direct relationship between wave frequency and form. Patterns and shapes of some materials occur only at specific frequencies.

In the Bible, however, there is not the orderly Egyptian process (i.e. God created the constituents of the world by calling the various "names"), but after creation occurred, the first human (Adam) called their names, as per Genesis 2:19:

> *God formed every beast of the field, and every fowl of the air; and brought them unto Adam to see what he would call them: <u>and whatsoever Adam called every living creature, that was the name thereof.</u>*

The above text from Genesis 2:19 shows that the biblical authors have confused two Ancient Egyptian **neteru** (gods)—**Atum/Atam** and **Thoth** (aka Tehuti). The above biblical verse, regarding the role of the first human, Adam, is very similar to what Diodorus of Sicily wrote about the Ancient Egyptian **neter**, **Thoth**, in *Book I*, [Section 16-1]:

> *It was by Thoth, according to Ancient Egyptians, that the common language of mankind was first further articulated, <u>and that many objects which were still nameless received an appellation, that the alphabet were defined,</u>...*

In the typical Egyptian story form, it was **Thoth** (Tehuti), who uttered the words, commanded by **Ra** (Re), that created the world. **Thoth** (Tehuti) is also referred to as the *Divine Tongue*, who gave names to the divine beings that resulted from the *Big Bang*—the first explosive sound that began the creation process.

The Big Bang that occurred about 15 billion years ago began building up the condensed energy in **Nun**—*the neutron soup* until it finally exploded and expanded outward. The explosion was loud enough to be called the *Big Bang*. The Ancient Egyptian texts likewise repeatedly stressed that sound was the cause of creation.

13.4 THE SIX DAYS OF CREATION

On The First Day (The Light)

> *God said, Let there be light: and there was light. And God saw the light... [and] divided the light from the darkness ...And the evening and the morning were the first day.* [Genesis 1:3-5]

The Division of Light from the Darkness was the first manifestation of creation. The Egyptians perceived the universe in terms of a dualism between the forces of Light and Darkness, i.e. **Ma-at**—*Truth and Order*—and disorder. The Creator summoned the cosmos out of undifferentiated chaos by distinguishing the two, and by giving voice to the ultimate ideal of Truth. On a cosmic level, it was manifested in the solar cycle in which the Creator had to repeatedly vanquish the forces of darkness every morning, as the sun rose—which is a constant theme in the Ancient Egyptian texts.

On the Second Day (The Firmament/Heavens)

> *God said, Let there be a firmament in the midst of the waters. And God made the firmament and divided the waters which were under the firmament from the waters which were above the firmament and it was so. And God called the firmament heaven.* [Genesis 1:6-8]

This biblical verse is badly mutilated Ancient Egyptian cosmology. We will explain this stage of creation in the Ancient Egyptian coherent way, in two segments as follows:

1. The biblical verses tell us that *"firmament arose from the waters"*. This was described in the Ancient Egyptian texts as the mound of creation rising out of the primeval cosmic ocean. This mound was called **Ben/BenBen/Bennu**. The action of a rising mound is indicative of the transformation from Subjective Being (**Nu/Ny/**

Nun) to Objective Being (**Atum/Atam**). In simple human terms, this is equivalent to the moment that one passes from sleeping (unconscious state/subjective being) to being aware of oneself (gaining consciousness/objective being). It is like standing on solid ground.

This stage of creation was represented by the Egyptian sages as **Atum/Atam** rising out of **Nu/Ny/Nun**. In the *Unas* (so-called *Pyramid*) *Texts*, there is the following invocation:

> *Salutation to thee, Atum, ...*
> *... Thou art high in this thy name High Mound. ...* [§1587]

It is interesting to note, here, the Ancient Egyptian origin of the biblical Adam. When the name, *Adam*, is written in the equivalent Ancient Egyptian alphabetical characters, it becomes **Atam/Atum**. In the Ancient Egyptian traditions, **Atam/Atum** represents the first realization of existence; and as such, he is depicted in full human form.

Atam/Atum means *he who completes or perfects*. In other words, **Atam** represents the Perfect Person.

2. Next, we can explain—in coherent Ancient Egyptian terms—the division of waters from the firmament, to be identified in Genesis as "heaven".

The Ancient Egyptian concept of the universe is like a box. The first thing the Divine created is a kind of bubble in what is otherwise an infinite ocean of water. The sky is the skin of the infinite ocean—that contains what we call the atmosphere, which was caused by two forces that the Ancient Egyptians called **Shu** and **Tefnut**. Both **Shu** (heat) and **Tefnut** (water) mean *atmosphere*. **Nun** (the pre-creation cosmic ocean) is the root out of which **Shu** and **Tefnut** were created.

Heat (**Shu**) and water (**Tefnut**) are the two most universal shaping factors of life forms. These terms correspond to fire (heat) and moisture, respectively, and are to be understood as metaphors and actual correspondences for the abstract qualities that they represent. **Shu**, represented by fire, air, and heat corresponds to the quality of expansiveness, rising, centrifugal forces, positive, masculine, outgoing, outward extroversion, etc. **Tefnut**, represented by moisture and the objective material basis of manifestation (**Nut**, the suffix), corresponds to contraction, downward movement, centripetal forces, negative, feminine, receptive, inner, introspection, etc.

The above Ancient Egyptian concept concurs with modern scientists, who tell us that the galaxies are subjected now to mainly two opposing forces: 1) *expulsion forces*, which cause all galaxies to move away from us, resulting from the effect of the *Big Bang*; and 2) *gravitational/contractional forces*, which pull the galaxies together.

We are still under the effect of the Big Bang, where the expulsion forces cause the galaxies to move away from us like an expanding bubble.

The outer limits of the expanding bubble are the firmament—the sky that is viewed poetically as a solid arch or vault depicted in Ancient Egypt as **Nut**.

On the Third Day: The Living Earth

> *9: And God said, Let the waters under the heaven be gathered together unto one place, and let the dry land appear: and it was so.*
> *10:And God called the dry land Earth; and the gathering together of the waters called he Seas: and God saw that it was good.*
> *11: And God said, Let the earth bring forth grass, the herb yielding seed, and the fruit tree yielding fruit after his kind,*

whose seed is in itself, upon the earth: and it was so.
12: And the earth brought forth grass, and herb yielding seed after his kind, and the tree yielding fruit, whose seed was in itself, after his kind: and God saw that it was good.
13: And the evening and the morning were the third day. [Genesis I, 9-13]

The above biblical verses miss an important point in the process of creation—namely the creation of the biosphere, which is essential to begin life on earth. In the Ancient Egyptian orderly process, once the atmosphere was created, it was possible for **Shu** (heat) and **Tefnut** (moisture) to beget **Geb** (Earth) and **Nut** (Sky), who by virtue of their separation, caused the space in which life could take place on earth. The Egyptian text in the *Bremner-Rhind Papyrus* describes the new life on earth:

I came forth from among the roots and I created all creeping things, and all that exists among them.

Similarly, animating the earth with divine energies (**neteru**) is stated clearly in the *Shabaka Stele* (8th Century BCE):

And so the neteru (gods) *entered into their bodies, in the form of every sort of wood, of every sort of mineral, as every sort of clay, as everything which grows upon him* (meaning earth).

On the Fourth Day: Stars, Sun, and Moon

14: And God said, Let there be <u>lights in the firmament of the heaven</u> to divide the day from the night; and let them be for signs, and for seasons, and for days, and years:
15: And let them be for lights in the firmament of the heaven to give light upon the earth: and it was so.
16: And <u>God made two great lights; the greater light to rule the day, and the lesser light to rule the night: he made the stars also.</u>
17: And God set them in the firmament of the heaven to give

light upon the earth,
18: And to rule over the day and over the night, and to divide
the light from the darkness: and God saw that it was good.
19: And the evening and the morning were the fourth day.
[Genesis I, 14-19]

"Lights in the firmament of the heaven" is depicted in Ancient Egypt as **Nut**—a star-studded woman arched over the heavens, in the act of swallowing the evening sun and giving birth to the morning sun.

Genesis I, 16, refers to the creation of the "greater light" of the day and the "lesser light" of the night. These "two lights" originated from Ancient Egyptian texts. In the Ancient Egyptian allegory of creation, the sun and moon are represented as the *two eyes*. The Ancient Egyptian allegory says that after **Shu** and **Tefnut** separated and left the cosmic ocean (**Nu/Nun**), the Divine sent his eye (Sun) to look for them in the extents of the **Nun**. Meanwhile, the Divine made another Eye—the Moon. This is a clever representation of how at night (when the Sun is gone), the Moon lights the sky.

The role of the two eyes (Sun and Moon) in the universe were described by Diodorus of Sicily, *Book I*, 11. 5-6,

> *... The sun contributing the fiery element and the spirit, the moon the wet and the dry, and both together the air; and it is through these elements that all things are engendered and nourished. And so it is out of the sun and moon that the whole physical body of the universe is made complete......*

On the Fifth Day: Animals and Birds

20: And God said, Let the waters bring forth abundantly the moving creature that hath life, and fowl that may fly above the earth in the open firmament of heaven.

21: And God created great whales, and every living creature that moveth, which the waters brought forth abundantly, after their kind, and every winged fowl after his kind: and God saw that it was good.

22: And God blessed them, saying, Be fruitful, and multiply, and fill the waters in the seas, and let fowl multiply in the earth.

23: And the evening and the morning were the fifth day.
[Genesis I, 20-23]

In Ancient Egyptian thinking, the creation of animals and birds is more than physical creation. Each animal/bird symbolizes and embodies certain divine functions and principles in a particularly pure and striking fashion. The chosen symbols for the various aspects of the Divine are embodied in the created creatures.

The animal or animal-headed **neteru** (gods/goddesses) are symbolic expressions of a deep spiritual understanding. When a total animal is depicted in Ancient Egypt, it represents a particular function/attribute in its purest form. When an animal-headed figure is depicted, it conveys that particular function/attribute in the human being. The two forms of Anubis, in the two illustrations shown above, clearly distinguish these two aspects. The dog embodies the essence of spiritual guidance. The dog/jackal is known for its reliable homing instinct, day or night. The dog is very useful in searches, and is the animal of choice to guide the blind. As such, it is an excellent choice for guiding the soul of the deceased through the regions of the Duat.

The metaphysical role of Anubis the dog is reflected in his diet. The dog/jackal feasts on carrion, turning it into beneficial nourishment. In other words: Anubis represents the capacity to turn waste into useful food for the body(and soul).

Several examples of animal symbolism can be found in *Egyptian Divinities: The All Who Are THE ONE*, by Moustafa Gadalla.

On the Sixth Day: Living Earth and Creation of Man

> *24: And God said, Let the earth bring forth the living creature after his kind, cattle, and creeping thing, and beast of the earth after his kind: and it was so.*
> *25: And God made the beast of the earth after his kind, and cattle after their kind, and every thing that creepeth upon the earth after his kind: and God saw that it was good.*
> *26: And God said, Let us make man in our image, after our likeness: and let them have dominion over the fish of the sea, and over the fowl of the air, and over the cattle, and over all the earth, and over every creeping thing that creepeth upon the earth.*
> *27: So God created man in his own image, in the image of God created he him; male and female created he them.*
> *28: And God blessed them, and God said unto them, Be fruitful, and multiply, and replenish the earth, and subdue it:*
> *31: And God saw every thing that he had made, and, behold, it was very good. And the evening and the morning were the sixth day.* [Genesis I, 24-31]

Genesis I, 24 sounds exactly like a text from the *Egyptian Book of Night*, which reads:

To come out of the Netherworld, to rest in the Morning Barge, to navigate the Abyss until the hour of Ra, She who sees the beauty of her Lord, to make transformations in Khepri, to rise to the horizon, to enter the mouth, to come out of the vulva, to burst forth out of the Gate of the Horizon of the Hour, She who lifts up the beauty of Ra in order to make live men, all cattle, all worms he has created.

Once land and sustenance were created, humanity was born.

It is commonly recognized by all theological and philosophical schools of thought that the human being is made in the image of God, i.e. a miniature universe; and that to understand the universe is to understand oneself, and vice versa.

Yet no culture has ever practiced the above principle like the Ancient Egyptians. Central to their complete understanding of the universe was the knowledge that man was made in the image of God and as such, man represented the image of all creation. Accordingly, Egyptian symbolism has always related to man. Here are two examples:

1. Man, to the Ancient Egyptians, was the embodiment of the laws of creation. As such, the physiological functions and processes of the various parts of the body were seen as manifestations of cosmic functions. The limbs and organs had a metaphysical function, in addition to their physical purpose. The parts of the body were consecrated to one of the **neteru** (divine principles), which appeared in the Egyptian records throughout its recovered history, such as from the *Papyrus of Ani*, [pl. 32, item 42]:

... there is no member of mine devoid of a neter (god, goddess) ...

2. Egyptians divided the sky into 36 sectors of ten degrees each, called decans. Osiris likewise has 36 forms. Like the sky, the human body, in Ancient Egyptian medicine, was also divided

into 36 sectors, and each came under the influence of a certain **neter/netert** (god/goddess), each controlled by one of the 36 parts of the Egyptian Zodiac. The Egyptian Zodiac consists of 12 months. Each month is divided into 3 segments of 10 days (like decans).

Man was lovingly formed by hand on God's potter's wheel, as per the well-known Ancient Egyptian depiction of **Khnum**, the Divine Potter, at his potter's wheel, fashioning men from clay [see an Ancient Egyptian depiction herein].

The same concept was echoed thousands of years later in Isaiah, 64:8:

> *Yet, O Lord, thou art our Father; we are the clay, and thou art our potter; we are all the work of thy hand.*

Passages of the Bible leave no doubt about the belief in the concept of the Divine Potter. Genesis 2:7 mentions the material used to make man, the same type of substance used by **Khnum**:

> *And the Lord God formed man of the dust of the ground, and breathed into his nostrils <u>the breath of life</u>; and man became a living soul.*

A passage from an Egyptian creation legend by **Khnum** follows:

The mud of the Nile, heated to excess by the Sun, fermented and generated, without seeds, the races of men and animals.

The term *breath of life* has special significance to the Ancient Egyptian, because it resonates on both the physical and spiritual levels. The breath of life is known in Ancient Egypt as **Amen/ Amon/Amun**. He represents the hidden or occult force underlying creation. The Ancient Egyptian papyrus known as the *Leyden Papyrus* describes **Amen** as:

He [who] gives birth to everything that is and causes all that exists to live.

The above biblical verse [Genesis 2:7], ***and breathed into his nostrils the breath of life; and man became a living soul*** describes a common Ancient Egyptian concept. In addition to animating each human body with the Divine Essence (Breath of Life), each statue, painting, relief or building in Ancient Egypt had to undergo this ritual upon its completion to ensure that it was transformed from an inanimate product of man's hands into a vibrant part of the divine order charged with numinous power.

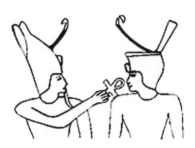

13.5 THE ANGELS OF GOD

The Ancient Egyptians believed in One God who was represented through the functions and attributes of "His" domain. These attributes were called the **neteru** (pronounced *neter-u*; masculine singular: **neter**; feminine singular: **netert**). There is an indefinite number of divinities (**neteru**) because the Divine has an endless number of aspects/attributes.

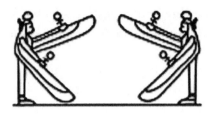

The **neteru** are the representation of universal principles, functions and attributes of the One Great and Supreme God. The **neteru** (who were called *'gods'* by some) were endorsed and incorporated into Christianity under a new name, *'angels'*.

The spheres of angels and archangels in Christianity are strikingly similar to Ancient Egypt's hierarchy of **neteru** (gods/goddesses). In many situations, the Ancient Egyptian **neteru** are depicted with wings, as Christianity would later do.

The Song of Moses in Deuteronomy (32:43), as found in a cave at Qumran, near the Dead Sea, mentions the word **'gods'** in the plural: *"**Rejoice, O heavens, with him; and do obeisance to him, ye gods.**"* When the passage is quoted in the New Testament (Hebrews 1:6), the word **'gods'** is substituted with 'angels of God'.

Upon careful examination, the concept of the Egyptian **neteru** was accepted by ancient and modern societies who merely chose new names to express Egyptian ideas.

13.6 TRINITIES IN ANCIENT EGYPT

The Ancient Egyptians recognized the significance of trinity in the creation process. This was eloquently illustrated in the Ancient Egyptian texts and traditions whereby the Self-Created begat **Shu** (heat) and **Tefnut** (moisture) then placed His arms around them, and His Essence entered into them, to become One again. It is the Three that are Two that are One. This is made clear in the Ancient Egyptian papyrus known as the *Bremner-Rhind Papyrus:*

After having become one neter (god), there were [now] three neteru (gods) in me ...

As such, Ancient Egyptian texts rendered the trinity as a unity expressed by the singular pronoun.

In the Ancient Egyptian texts, **Shu** and **Tefnut** are described as the ancestors of all the **neteru** (gods/goddesses) who begat all beings in the universe. This first trinity ensured a continuous relationship between the Creator and all subsequent created.

[For more information about examples of familiar Ancient Egyptian trinities and their interrelationships see *Egyptian Divinities* by Moustafa Gadalla.]

The trinity was a major preoccupation of Egyptian theologians that extended to every aspect of existence. The Ancient Egyptians realized the physical and metaphysical role of Trinity, for each unity has a *triple power* and a *double nature*. A few examples of the Egyptians' implementation of this realization are:

1. Each Ancient Egyptian temple has a triple shrine to enshrine the three powers (three **neteru**) of each temple.

2. Each small locality in Ancient Egypt had its own trinity of **neteru**.

3. In the Ancient Egyptian numerology, **Ausar** (Osiris) represents the number 3.

CHAPTER 14 : THE ANCIENT EGYPTIAN/ CHRISTIAN HOLIDAYS

14.1 THE NEED FOR RENEWAL/REBIRTH

The main theme of the Ancient Egyptian texts is the cyclical nature of the universe and the constant need for the renewal of such cycles through well designated festivals.

The Egyptians viewed/view these festivals as part of human existence, which constitutes the rhythm of the life of the community and the individual. This rhythm results from the order of cosmic life.

The renewal and rejuvenation of the life of the cosmos, of the community, and of the individual are affected by rites. These rites had/have the power to bring about the rejuvenation and rebirth of divine life. As such, the Ancient (and present-day) Egyptian festivals came to have the function of enactments of cosmological (religious) renewals.

During numerous Ancient Egyptian religious festivals, the participants fall back on the archetypal truth of their cosmic consciousness—*As above so below, and as below so above.* Every holy festival actualizes the archetypal holy cycle. These holy cycles have become part of the calendar. More accurately, the calendar served to indicate when the cosmological powers (**neteru**) were manifested, as well as their renewal cycles. All early Greek and

Roman writers affirmed this Ancient Egyptian tradition, such as Plutarch, in his *Moralia Vol. V* [377,65]:

> *... They [the Egyptians] associate theological concepts with the seasonal changes in the surrounding atmosphere, or with the growth of the crops and seed-times and plowing ...*

14.2 SETTING THE DATES (REJUVENATION CYCLES)

From the records of early historians, such as Plutarch, Herodotus and Diodorus, as well as the hundreds of festival records throughout Ancient Egypt, it is clear that setting the dates of these festivals was synchronized with cosmological rhythms. Setting the dates of both ancient and present-day festivals were/ are subject to three cycles, individually or a combination of two or all three. The three cycles are:

1. The solar cycle which commands the seasons with all that that implies.

2. The lunar cycle that governs fertility and other biological periodicities, as well as the various meteorological phenomena.

3. The day of the week, which is related to the seven planets and the seven musical notes.

As a consequence of utilizing a combination of the three cycles, many festival dates may vary widely from year to year—just like the Easter celebration, which is also determined according to the three Egyptian elements: a weekday that follows a full moon, which follows the vernal equinox (i.e. solar cycle).

Some significant points about the Egyptian cyclical calendar of events (past or present) include:

• There are several related festivals that are observed in certain cyclical sequences, and as such are separated by a set period. Some festivals are spaced at specific cycles such as 7, 40, or 50 days from other more prominent events. Each of these cycles has its own significance. A comparable example in the Christian ecclesiastical calendar is Easter, which is tied to Lent, Ascension Day, and Pentecost.

• The 40-day cycle signifies the time to die or to be reborn. The Egyptians believe that it takes 40 days to die (prior to actual death) and 40 days (after actual death) for the soul to leave the body completely. Consequently, the mummification (body dehydration) period lasted 40 days.

• 50 days is associated with renewal. This was illustrated in the Ancient Egyptian model story when Seth, after disposing of Osiris, ruled as a tyrant for 50 "days" before Seth was replaced by Horus representing the resurrection/renewal of Osiris.

14.3 THE BULL OF HIS MOTHER

One of the most important rituals in the Egyptian annual festivals since ancient times is the ritual sacrifice of the bull, which represents the renewal of the cosmic forces through the death and resurrection of the bull-neter (god).

In Ancient Egypt, the Mother-netert (goddess), Isis, had a son who, in the form of a bull, was sacrificed annually in order to assure the cycle of the seasons and the continuity of Nature.

As per present practices, ancient writers asserted that it was the mother who was chosen to produce a calf with particular qualities—he was *The Bull of His Mother* so to speak. Herodotus, in describing him, says:

> *Apis, also called Epaphus, is a young bull whose mother can have no other offspring, and who is reported by the Egyptians*

to conceive from lightning sent from heaven, and thus to produce the bull-god Apis.

The religious connotations of this sacrifice are an echo of a sacrifice in the sacrament, where we are reminded of Christ's death so that mankind might be saved. In essence, this is a genuine religious drama in which, as in the Catholic Mass, a god is worshiped and sacrificed.

Diodorus, in *Book I* [85, 3-5], explains the rejuvenation powers of the sacrificial bull,

> **Some explain the origin of the honor accorded this bull in this way, saying that at the death of Osiris his soul passed into this animal, and therefore up to this day <u>he always passed into its successors at the times of the manifestation of Osiris.</u>**

Osiris represents the process, growth, and the underlying cyclical aspects of the universe—the principle that makes life come from apparent death.

Osiris represents the rejuvenation/renewal principle in the universe. Therefore, in the Ancient Egypt context, the bull had to suffer a sacrificial death to ensure the life of the community. The sacrifice of the holy animal, and the eating of his flesh, brought about a state of grace.

It continues to be a common practice in present-day Egypt that young bulls are sacrificed upon the death of a person. The same practice continues in thousands of annual folk saints' festivals in Egypt.

The traditions of bull rituals and sacrifices were observed in Egypt prior to any other country, as testified by classical Greek and Roman writers.

14.4 FAMILIAR ANCIENT EGYPTIAN/CHRISTIAN FESTIVALS

The following samples of familiar Ancient/modern Egyptian festivals shows that the Christian annual festivals are adopted from Ancient Egyptian festivals.

The dates provided in the sample festivals are based on the Ancient Egyptian calendar (which is still in use under the name *Coptic Calendar*), as well as the equivalent date in the "Latin" calendar.

14.5 THE LAST SUPPER

Earlier, when we presented the Isis and Osiris allegory, we referred to how Osiris was invited by Seth to a feast where Seth and his accomplices tricked Osiris into laying down in a makeshift coffin, closed and sealed the chest, and threw it into the Nile. Seth became the new Pharaoh as the coffin containing the lifeless body of Osiris flowed into the Mediterranean Sea. The date of such a (symbolic) event was given by Plutarch, in his *Moralia, Vol. V* (356),

> *... and those who were in the plot ran to it and slammed down the lid, which they fastened by nails from the outside.*
> *... They say also that the date on which this deed was done was the 17th day of Athor* [27 **November**], *when the sun passes through Scorpion.*

The events of 17 **Hatoor**/Athor (27 November), as reported by Plutarch, have all the elements of the biblical Jesus' Last Supper, i.e. a conspiracy, feast, friends, and betrayal.

The *Loss of* Osiris is now celebrated in the *Abu Sefein* (reference to Osiris' two emblems—the crook and the flail) *Festival* in Egypt at the same date and with the same traditions, i.e. a big feast followed by a 40-day cycle of figurative death by fasting and other disciplinary means.

28 days after the Last Supper is the birth/re-birth of the renewed king on 25 December.

40 days after the Last Supper is Epiphany (6 January).

14.6 ADVENT AND CHRISTMAS

Osiris' life, being a symbol of the moon [see Chapter 13], is associated with a cycle of 28 days (4 weeks). This was echoed later in the Christian Advent, which in Latin is *ad-venio*, meaning *to come to*. The *Catholic Encyclopedia* admits that: *"Advent is a period embracing 4 Sundays. The first Sunday may be as early as 27 November, and then Advent has 28 days."* As noted above, 27 November is the date of the symbolic *Last Supper, Death,* and *Loss of Osiris.*

The 28-day cycle of Osiris and its relationship to the regeneration principle is nicely depicted in the famed scene of the resurrection of the wheat, which depicts Osiris with 28 stalks of wheat growing out of his coffin.

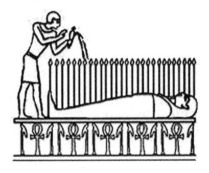

The ecclesiastical year begins with Advent in the Western churches. According to the *Catholic Encyclopedia*, "the faithful are admonished, during this time:

• To prepare themselves worthily to celebrate the anniversary of the Lord coming into the world as the incarnate God of love,

• Thus to make their souls fitting abodes for the Redeemer coming in Holy Communion and through grace, and

• Thereby to make themselves ready for His final coming as judge, at death and at the end of the world."

All the above elements are of Ancient Egyptian origin. Such traditions were observed during (and in fact were based on) the annual jubilee of the Ancient Egyptian King, known as the **Sed** (or **Heb-Sed**) Festival, which was always held during the month of Kee-hek (Khoiakh, i.e. December) every year. This festival dates from time immemorial, and continued to be celebrated throughout the Ancient Egyptian history.

The intent of this annual event was the renewal/rejuvenation of the supernatural powers of the King. The renewal rituals aimed at bringing a new life force to the King, i.e. a (figurative) death and a (figurative) rebirth of the reigning King. In the Ancient Egyptian traditions, this concept of perpetual power (between the old and the new) is eloquently illustrated and shown earlier in this book in the depiction of Horus being born out of Osiris, after Osiris death. This gives more meaning to the phrase: *The King is dead—Long live the King.*

In the Ancient Egyptian traditions, the rejuvenation/birthday of a new/renewed King comes symbolically 28 days after 27 November—the symbolic *Last Supper* and the *Death of* Osiris—i.e. 25 December. The Christian calendar celebrates the same day as the birth (rebirth) of the new King, namely Jesus, who is referred to as a King throughout the Bible. The 28-day cycle signifies the Advent (both in Ancient Egyptian and Christian traditions) of the *King*.

All the elements mentioned in the *Catholic Encyclopedia* on the previous page concur with their Egyptian origin, whereby Osiris incarnates as Horus, and that Osiris is the judge of the dead.

Due to the absolute lack of historical and archaeological evidence to support the biblical accounts of Jesus, the church fathers turned to Egypt to pick some dates from a list that was attributed to Clement of Alexandria. The list places several dates: 25 Pachon (20 May) and 24 or 25 Pharmuthi (19 or 20 April). Clement, however, indicated that Epiphany (and with it, probably the Nativity) was celebrated on 15 or 11 of Tobi (10 or 6 January). 6 January is proven to be the date adopted for his "birthday" throughout the various churches in the Mediterranean Basin. 25 December came later and was based on the Julian calendar, which is 13 days behind 6 January. [See the explanation of the 13-day difference in Appendix E of *Egyptian Mystics: Seekers of the Way*, by same author.]

14.7 THE KING'S NEW YEAR'S DAY (JANUARY 1)

As stated earlier, typical Egyptian festivals extend for an octave-week. As such, the Egyptian King's renewal day of 25 December (Julian calendar) has its climax in its octave (8 days later) on 1 January—the New Year's Day for the rejuvenated King. On the 22nd of Kee-hek/Khoiakh (1 January), during the annual jubilee festivities, a special ceremony was held, at which a ceremonial voyage was led by the effigy of Osiris, accompanied by 34 images of divinities in 34 little boats illuminated by 365 candles (the candles represent the number of days in a regular year).

When Julius Caesar came to Egypt in 48 BCE, he commissioned the astronomer Sosigenes (from Alexandria) to introduce a calendar into the Roman Empire. This resulted in the Julian calendar of 365 days a year and 366 days every leap year. The Roman (Julian) calendar was literally tailored to be fit for a King. The first day of the year was the coronation day for the Egyptian King at the end of the annual rejuvenation Jubilee—the **Heb-Sed** Festivals.

14.8 EPIPHANY (JANUARY 6)

A cycle of 40 days after the Egyptian Last Supper (27 November) and the death of Osiris was/is the Epiphany on 6 January, which was later adopted in the Christian calendar of events for the same objective.

Like the Ancient Egyptian traditions, the original intent of Epiphany in the Eastern Church is for one about to be baptized—the sacrament of Baptism. As stated earlier, baptism represents figurative death and rebirth. A born-again cycle typically takes 40 days (from 27 November to 6 January). At the end of the cycle, the people bathe in the Nile (baptism), and the fast is broken. Happy days are here again.

Baladi Egyptians (who were forced to be Moslems) continue to celebrate this occasion because it is an Ancient Egyptian tradition that was later adopted by the Christians.

14.9 LENT

Lent denotes the 40 days' fast that precedes the Holy Week of Easter. One has to (figuratively) die in order to be (figuratively) reborn. Lent represents the figurative death (fasting, self-discipline, etc.) before rebirth.

Lent and Easter pre-date Christianity, as explained below. Lent was, in origin, the time of the final preparation for candidates for the solemn rite of baptism at the Easter Vigil. The ritual of baptism was performed in the sacred lakes of the Ancient Egyptian temples and in the River Nile itself.

14.10 EASTER

It has been common knowledge that the Christian Easter was not a historical event, but that the festival preceded Christianity. The Webster's dictionary describes Easter as the "*name of pagan vernal festival almost coincident in date with paschal festival of the church"*. The so-called *"pagan"* festival is the Egyptian Easter. In the Egyptian (and later the Christian) calendar, Easter is the center of the greater part of the ecclesiastical year—from Septuagesima to the last Sunday after Pentecost, the feast of the Ascension, Pentecost, Corpus Christi, and all other movable feasts—because they are tied to the Easter date.

Commemorating Easter is the cornerstone upon which the Christian faith is built. Yet the Apostolic Fathers do not mention it because it was a continuation of an existing Jewish holiday—namely Passover—which in turn was/is an adoption of an Ancient Egyptian Spring festival.

Ancient Egyptian records indicate that the Egyptian Spring Festival was in existence for over 5,000 years. The purpose of such festival was/is the renewal of nature in the springtime, when life returns once more to the world.

As stated earlier, Osiris represents the cyclical nature of the universe, the principle that makes life come from apparent death. It was therefore natural that Osiris be identified with Spring—of the day when he was believed to have risen from the dead.

More than 5,000 years ago, Ancient Egyptians adopted a national holiday, which came at the end of an 8-day festival. According to Egyptian allegory, Osiris died, was buried and then disappeared on the fifth day—Friday Eve. They called that day the *Loss of Osiris*. Osiris was resurrected three days later, i.e. on Sunday, as the judge (king) of the dead.

As is the case of the Egyptian Osiris, the Christian Easter reflects the Christian conviction that Christ died, was buried, and subsequently disappeared on Friday; and was resurrected the third day after his death, on Sunday. It is the happiest day in the Christian calendar.

The Easter celebration, like all Egyptian festivals, lasts an octaveweek (known in the Christian calendar as the Holy Week, extending from Palm Sunday to Easter Sunday). The Ancient Egyptian Holy Week is followed by Easter Monday—known in Egypt as *Sham en Neseem*. This is the only official national holiday that has survived uninterrupted since Ancient Egyptian times.

14.11 ASCENSION DAY

In the Ancient Egyptian tradition, the spirit of the deceased takes 40 days to completely depart the body and ascend to the heavens. Accordingly, the mummification (body dehydration) period lasted 40 days. Likewise, the Christian calendar commemorates Ascension Day on the 40th day after Easter, when it celebrates *"the bodily ascent of Jesus into Heaven, on the 40th day after resurrection"*.

14.12 THE EGYPTIAN PENTECOST

The *Apostles (Prophets)* annual Festival in Egypt is held 50 days after Easter. Likewise, in the Christian calendar, the faithful celebrate Pentecost, which happens 50 days after Easter. Pentecost celebrates *"the descent of the Holy Spirit upon the Apostles"*.

This festival is of Ancient Egyptian origin. Pentecost signifies the period of the *Khamaseen* (meaning T*he Fifty*) when the southerly hot and reddish sandstorms and winds are of frequent occurrence. This annual event commences on the day immediately following Good Friday (Easter [Light] Saturday), and ceases on the Day of Pentecost (or Whitesunday)—an interval of 50 days.

This Pentecostal event is related to the Ancient Egyptian allegory about Isis and Osiris. The 50-day period represents the oppressive rule of Seth, after Osiris was dethroned. Seth represents the color red and the oppressive weather that is dry, fiery, and arid. In essence, Seth represents the red, hot cloud of dust—*Khamaseen*.

The allegory continues that as soon as Horus had grown to manhood, he challenged Seth for the right to the throne. After several battles between them, they went to the council of the 12 neteru (gods, goddesses) to determine who should rule. The council decided that Osiris/Horus should regain the throne of Egypt, and Seth should rule over the deserts/wastelands. In weather terms, this decision by the council ended the 50 days of oppressive weather (the *Khamaseen*). The date of judgment by the council of neteru/apostles/prophets was declared to be Whitesunday (White-Sunday), meaning the 50 reddish days are over; it's all clear, now.

14.13 TRANSFIGURATION OF HORUS/CHRIST

After Osiris ascended to the heavens, Isis began weeping. The Eve of the 11th of the Ancient Egyptian month of Ba-oo-neh (18 June) is called *"Leylet en-Nuktah"* (or the *Night of the Tear Drop*), as it commemorates the first drop that falls into the Nile, to begin the annual Nile flood season.

Fifty days after Isis' first teardrop (on 17 June), on 6 August, the Ancient Egyptians celebrated the reappearance of Osiris in the form of the resurrected Horus. This was confirmed by Plutarch in his *Moralia Vol. V* (372,52B):

> *In the sacred hymns of Osiris they call upon him who is hidden in the arms of the Sun; and on the <u>thirtieth of the month Epiphi</u> [6 August] they celebrate the birthday of the <u>Eyes of Horus</u>, at the time when the Moon and the Sun are in a perfectly straight line, since they regard not only the Moon but also the Sun as the eye and light of Horus.*

This is identical with the later Christians' claim of the transfiguration of Jesus, celebrated by the Orthodox church on 6 August. This holiday commemorates the *"revelation of Jesus' divinity to Peter, James, and John"*.

This Ancient Egyptian tradition continues, camouflaged in the

Mouled of El-Desouki, at the town of Desouk, on the east bank of the westerly branch of the Nile River. El-Desouki is lovingly known as *Abu-el-e-nane* (of the two eyes), just like *Horus the Elder of the Two Eyes.*

This annual Egyptian festival is recognized by the best magical (divination) acts in Egypt, which corresponds to the later Christian celebration whose main theme is the "revelation of (Jesus) divinity".

14.14 OUR LADY MERIAM (ASSUMPTION OF OUR LADY DAY)

The 15th day of August is a national holiday in many countries, commemorating the Ascension of the Virgin Mary to the heavens after her death. On the very same day—15 August- the Egyptians have been commemorating, since ancient times, a very similar festival that relates to the (symbolic) death of the Ancient Egyptian Virgin Mother, called *Bride of the Nile.*

In the Ancient Egyptian context, the *Bride of the Nile* is Isis, the Virgin Mother, and the River Nile is her soul mate, Osiris. On 15 August, the Ancient Egyptian festival commemorates the end of the 50-day rainy period in Ethiopia, which causes the annual flooding of the Nile.

The Egyptians associate the beginning of the annual flood season with Isis, who began to weep after her soul-mate, namely Osiris, ascended to heaven 40 days after his death. Egyptians associated Isis' first teardrop with the beginning of the rise of the Nile. Isis continued to weep, wishing for the lifeless Osiris to rise again. The *Weeping Widow* became, for the Egyptians, the *Lady of Sorrow.*

One of the most compelling parts of this Egyptian popular folktale is how these two symbols relate to the flood season in Egypt. The beauty here is that Isis wishes for Osiris (symbolizing the

water) to rise from his coma, and the water of the Nile consequently rise as a result of her weeping.

Isis therefore recreates/regenerates Osiris from her tears every
year. Her tears are blood-red in color, which is the same color of
the floodwaters, since this water comes as a result of the rainy
season in Ethiopia which erodes the silt of the Ethiopian high-
lands and carries it towards Egypt along the Blue Nile and other
tributaries. So, Isis' tears represent this reddish color of the water
during the flood season. In essence, Isis is crying a river—so to
speak. The Christian faithfulls follow the same Ancient Egyptian traditions in their presentations of the statue of Mary with
bloody teardrops coming out of her eyes.

In this popular Egyptian allegory, Isis finished her crying over
her soul mate, Osiris in about the middle of August, which means
that Isis cried all the tears she had. It is at this point in time that
the Egyptians (both ancient and modern) hold a festival, signifying the last teardrop from Isis, which will cause the peak of the
flood level. It is during this celebration that the Egyptians throw
an effigy of Isis into the waters to symbolize that Isis drowned in
her own tears—the River Nile itself.

In addition to the official governmental celebrations, the *Baladi*
Egyptians hold an annual festival called *Sitena Meriam* (meaning:
Our Lady Meriam). This is not a "Christian festival". The festival
lasts the typical Egyptian octaveweek (8 days). It begins on 15
August and ends on 16 Mesoree (22 August).

14.15 ISIS' (MARY'S) BIRTHDAY

The Ancient Egyptians followed the Sothic year, a period of
365.25636 days. Besides the adjustments made for the 0.00636
days per year [see details in Appendix E of our book, *Egyptian
Mystics: Seekers of the Way*], the Ancient Egyptians divided the
year into 12 equal months of 30 days each and added five (plus
one every 4 years) extra days. These extra days currently begin

on 6 September. In the typical Egyptian story form, five **neteru** (gods) were born on each of the five days—Osiris, Isis, Seth, Horus Behdety (Apollo), and Hathor.

The Nativity of the Virgin Mary is celebrated in the church on the Eve of 8 September, which is Isis' "birthday" as the second of 5 deities born in the 5 "extra days".

> **40 days after Isis' (Mary's) birthday is the Egyptian Conception (Planting) Annual Festival.**

> **40 days after planting the seeds, the Egyptians celebrated/celebrate the event of the Last Supper and the Loss of Osiris.**

And the orderly observation of cycles goes on, to maintain synchronism between the Below (on earth) and the Above (in heaven).

GLOSSARY

Amarna Letters – The Amarna letters were discovered in 1887, in the Amarna region. They consist of a collection of several hundred clay tablets written in cuneiform. The letters were sent to Akhenaton and Amenhotep III from other kings and rulers of the adjoining lands. Egypt's replies to these letters were never found, so we have only one side of the correspondence. By inference, however, it is quite possible to guess many subject matters of concern.

Amen/Amun/Amon – represents the hidden or occult force underlying creation. **Amen** represents the spirit that animates the universe with all its constituents and, as such, he is the reason why the whole universe exists. In the creative aspect, he is identified with **Re**, as **Amen-Re**.

Baladi – The term *Baladi* denotes the present silent majority of Egyptians that adhere to the Ancient Egyptian traditions, with a thin exterior layer of Islam. The Christian population of Egypt is an ethnic minority that came as refugees from Judaea and Syria to the Ptolemaic/Romanruled Alexandria. Now, 2,000 years later, they are easily distinguishable in looks and mannerisms from the majority of native Egyptians. [See *Ancient Egyptian Culture Revealed,* by Moustafa Gadalla, for detailed information. Also see Copt. *BCE* – **B**efore **C**ommon **E**ra. Also noted in other references as BC.]

Book of Coming Forth By Light (**Per-em-hru**) – consists of over 100 chapters of varying lengths, which are closely related to the so-called *Pyramid Texts* at Saqqara. These texts are found on papyrus scrolls that were wrapped in the mummy swathings of the deceased and buried with him.

Book of the Dead – see *Book of Coming Forth By Light*.

CE – Common Era. Also noted in other references as AD.

Copt – is derived from the Greek rendering for an *Egyptian*. The Arabs, after 641 CE, labeled only the Christian population as *Copts*. As a result, the term '*Coptic*' took on a different meaning by the 7th century.

cosmology – The study of the origin, creation, structure, and orderly operation of the universe as a whole, and of its related parts.

Dead Sea Scrolls – the remains of the library of the Essenes, a secret Jewish sect that separated itself from the Jewish community at large and from the Jerusalem priesthood, whose beliefs and teachings they regarded as false. Some of the manuscripts, found in a series of caves at Qumran early in 1947, were in Hebrew and Aramaic and some, in Greek scripts, have been dated between 200 BCE and 50 CE, and include biblical and sectarian texts. They also include Jewish literature and other documents.

Heb-Sed – Ancient Egyptian annual festival associated with the rejuvenation of the spiritual and physical powers of the Pharaoh.

mysticism – consists of ideas and practices that lead to *union with the Divine*. Union is described more accurately as *togetherness, joining, arriving, conjunction*, and the *realization of God's uniqueness*.

neter/netert – a divine principle/function/attribute of the One Great God. Incorrectly translated as *god/goddess*.

ostracon – Term used by archaeologists to refer to shards of pottery or flakes of limestone bearing texts and drawings.

papyrus – could mean either: 1) A plant that is used to make a writing surface. 2) *Paper*, as a writing medium. 3) The text written on it, such as *"Leyden Papyrus"*.

Pyramid Texts – a collection of transformational (funerary) literature that was found in the tombs of the 5th and 6th Dynasties (2465-2150 BCE).

Re – represents the primeval, cosmic, creative force. His hidden name is **Amen**, which means *secret*. All **neteru** (gods/goddesses) who took part in the creation process are aspects of **Re**. Therefore, **Re** is often linked with other **neteru**, such as **Atum-Re**, **Re-Harakhte**, etc.

stele (plural: *stelae*) – stone or wooden slab or column inscribed with commemorative texts.

Talmud – The most important work of religious law in post-biblical Judaism, composed in Babylon and Palestine between the 1st and 5th centuries CE.

Thomas (Gospel of) – One of the Coptic gospels found in Nag Hammadi, which includes many previously unknown sayings of Christ.

Thoth – represents the Divine aspects of wisdom and intellect. It was Thoth who uttered the words that created the world, as commanded by **Re**. He is represented as the messenger of the **neteru** (gods/goddesses) of writing, language, and knowledge.

SELECTED BIBLIOGRAPHY

Blackman, Aylward M. *Gods, Priests and Men: Studies in the Religion of Pharaonic Egypt.* London and New York, 1998.

Bleeker, C.J. *Egyptian Festivals: Enactments of Religious Renewal.* Leiden, 1967.

Breasted, James Henry. *A History of Egypt.* New York, 1924.

The Dawn of Conscience. New York, 1933.

Ancient Records of Egypt, vol. 3. Chicago, 1906.

Budge, Sir E.A. Wallis. *Egyptian Religion: Egyptian Ideas of Future Life.* London, 1975.

The Gods of the Egyptians (2 vols). New York, 1969.

Osiris and the Egyptian Resurrection (2 vols). New York, 1973.

The Egyptian Heaven and Hell (3 vols). London, 1976.

Campbell, Joseph. *The Hero with a Thousand Faces.* London, 1949.

The Power of Myth. North Carolina, USA, 1991.

Carter, Howard and A.C. Mace. *The Discovery of the Tomb of Tutankhamen.* New York, 1977.

The Tomb of Tutankhamen. Cassell, London, 1933.

Catholic Encyclopedia, Online Edition, 1999. http://www.newadvent.org/cathen/.

Conder, C.R. *The Tell Amarna Tablets*. London, 1893.

Cott, Jonathan. *Isis and Osiris*. New York, 1994.

Diodorus, Sicilus. *Vol 1*. Tr. by C.H. Oldfather. London, 1964.

Edwards, I.E.S. *Tutankhamun's Jewelry*. London, 1979.

Erman, Adolf. *Life in Ancient Egypt*. New York, 1971.

Freud, Sigmund. *Moses and Monotheism*. London, 1951.

Gadalla, Moustafa. *Egyptian Cosmology: The Animated Universe, 2nd ed.* Greensboro, NC, U.S.A., 2001.

  Egyptian Divinities: The ALL Who Are THE ONE. Greensboro, NC, U.S.A., 2001.

  Exiled Egyptians: The Heart of Africa. Greensboro, NC, U.S.A., 1999.

  Historical Deception, The Untold Story of Ancient Egypt, 2nd ed. Greensboro, NC, U.S.A., 1999.

  Egyptian Mystics: Seekers of the Way. Greensboro, NC, U.S.A., 2003.

  Egyptian Romany: The Essence of Hispania. Greensboro, NC, U.S.A., 2004.

  Tut-Ankh-Amen: The Living Image of the Lord. Erie, PA, U.S.A., 1997.

Greek Orthodox Archdiocese of America website. www.goarch.org. 2002.

Harpur, Tom. *The Pagan Christ: Recovering the Lost Light*. Toronto, Canada, 2004.

Herodotus. *The Histories*. Tr. By Aubrey DeSelincourt. London, 1996.

Josephus, Flavius. *Against Apion*, tr. H. St J. Thackeray. London, 1926.

The Antiquities of the Jews, 9 vols. Cambridge, MA, USA, 1965.

The Jewish War. New York, 1959.

Kennedy, H.A.A. *St. Paul and the Mystery Religions.* London, 1969.

Kenyon, Kathleen M. *The Bible and Recent Archaeology*, rev. ed. by P.R.S. Moorey. London, 1987.

Kuhn, Alvin Boyd. *A Rebirth for Christianity.* Theosophical Publishing House, 1970.

The Root of All Religion. Kila, MT, 1993.

Massey, Gerald. *Ancient Egypt.* New York, 1970.

Ancient Egypt, The Light of the World: A Work of Reclamation and Restitution in Twelve Volumes, vols. 1, 2. Kila, MT, 2001.

The Historical Jesus and the Mythical Christ. Kila, MT, 2002.

The Natural Genesis. Kila, MT, 1999.

Mowry, Lucetta. *The Dead Sea Scrolls and the Early Church.* Chicago, 1962.

Osman, Ahmed. *The House of the Messiah.* London, 1994.

Moses, Pharaoh of Egypt. London, 1991.

Out of Egypt: The Roots of Christianity Revealed. London, 1998.

Stranger in the Valley of the Kings. London, 1989.

Pagels, Elaine. *The Gnostic Gospels.* New York, 1979. *The Gnostic Paul.* Philadelphia, PA, USA, 1992.

Adam, Eve and the Serpent. New York, 1988. *The Origin of Satan.* New York, 1996.

Plutarch. *Plutarch's Moralia, Volume V*. Tr. by Frank Cole Babbitt. London, 1927.

Polano, H. *Selections from the Talmud.* London, 1894

Robinson, James M., ed. *The Nag Hammadi Library.* New York, 1978.

Sicilus, Diodorus. *see* Diodorus, Sicilus.

Vermes, Geza. *The Dead Sea Scrolls in English.* London, 1987.

Yadin, Yigael. *Hazor.* London, 1975.

Yahuda, A.S. *The Language of the Pentateuch in its Relation to Egyptian.* Oxford, 1933.

—————. *The Egyptian Book of the Dead.* New York, 1967.

—————. *Jewish Encyclopedia*, managing editor Isidore Singer. New York and London, 1904.

SOURCES AND NOTES

References to sources in the previous section, *Selected Bibliography,* are only referred to for facts, events, and dates—not for their interpretations of such information.

It should be noted that if a reference is made to one of the author Moustafa Gadalla's books, that each of his book contains appendices for its own extensive bibliography as well as detailed Sources and Notes.

Part I—The Ancestors of the Christ King

Chapter 1: The Historical Christ's Royal Ancestors

Son of the Highest – Bible

The Historicity of the Bible – Osman (*Stranger in the Valley of the Kings*), Gadalla (*Historical Deception, 2nd ed., Tut-Ankh-Amen*)

Chapter 2: David and Tut Homosis III

(I) His Youth –

Biblical Account – Osman (*The House of the Messiah*), Gadalla (*Historical Deception, Tut-Ankh-Amen*), Bible

Twthomosis III As A Youth – Osman (*The House of the Messiah*), Gadalla (*Historical Deception, Tut-Ankh-Amen*)

(II) The Biblical Warrior King – Osman (*The House of the Messiah*), Gadalla (*Historical Deception, Tut-Ankh-Amen*), Bible

The Egyptian Warrior King – Osman (*The House of the Messiah*), Gadalla (*Historical Deception, Tut-Ankh-Amen*)

Chapter 3: Solomon and Amenhotep III

General – Osman (*The House of the Messiah*), Gadalla (*Historical Deception, Tut-Ankh-Amen*), Bible

Coronation of the King – Osman (*The House of the Messiah*), Gadalla (*Historical Deception, Tut-Ankh-Amen*), Bible

The Great Builder – Osman (*The House of the Messiah*), Gadalla (*Historical Deception, Tut-Ankh-Amen*), Bible, Kenyon, Yadin

The Wisdom of the King – Osman (*The House of the Messiah*), Gadalla (*Historical Deception, Tut-Ankh-Amen*), Bible

Chapter 4: Moses and Akhenaton

Monotheism and Monomania – See detailed information throughout chapter.

Freud and Moses – Osman (*Moses: Pharaoh of Egypt*), Gadalla (*Historical Deception, Tut-Ankh-Amen*), Bible, Freud

Aton Worship – Osman (*Stranger in the Valley of the Kings, Moses: Pharaoh of Egypt*), Gadalla (*Historical Deception, Tut-Ankh-Amen*), Bible

The Ruler – Osman (*Moses: Pharaoh of Egypt, The House of the Messiah*), Gadalla (*Historical Deception, Tut-Ankh-Amen*), Bible, Conder

The Exile – Osman (*Moses: Pharaoh of Egypt*), Gadalla (*Historical Deception, Tut-Ankh-Amen*), Polano

The Death of Moses/Akhenaton – Osman (*Moses: Pharaoh of Egypt*), Gadalla (*Historical Deception, Tut-Ankh-Amen*), Bible, Polano

Part II—The Historical Christ King

Chapter 5: Jesus and History

The Jesus of History – Osman (*The House of the Messiah*), Bible, Gadalla (*Historical Deception, Tut-Ankh-Amen*), Baigent

The Historical Absence and the Gospels Prominence – Osman (*The House of the Messiah, Out of Egypt*), Bible, Gadalla (*Historical Deception, Tut-Ankh-Amen*), Polano, Josephus

Moses and Jesus of the Same Era – Osman (*The House of the Messiah*), Gadalla (*Historical Deception, Tut-Ankh-Amen*), Polano, Josephus

Jesus the Gnostic Nazarenes – Osman (*The House of the Messiah*), Gadalla (Historical *Deception, Tut-Ankh-Amen*), Bible, Polano, Baigent

Chapter 6: His Epithets

The Living Image of the Lord – Osman (*The House of the Messiah*), Gadalla (*Historical Deception, Tut-Ankh-Amen*), Bible

Christ – Osman (*The House of the Messiah*), Gadalla (*Historical Deception, Tut-Ankh-Amen*), Bible

Messiah – Osman (*The House of the Messiah*), Gadalla (*Historical Deception, Tut-Ankh-Amen*), Bible

Jesus/Joshua – Osman (*The House of the Messiah*), Gadalla (*Historical Deception, Tut-Ankh-Amen*), Bible

Immanuel – Osman (*The House of the Messiah*), Gadalla (*Historical Deception, Tut-Ankh-Amen*), Bible

Ben Pandira (Son of God) – Osman (*The House of the Messiah*), Gadalla (*Historical Deception, Tut-Ankh-Amen*), Bible, Polano

Chapter 7: The Divine Man

The Biblical Jesus–The Divine Son – Osman (*The House of the Messiah*), Gadalla (*Historical Deception, Tut-Ankh-Amen*), Bible

Twt-Ankh-Amen–The Divine Son – Osman (*The House of the Messiah*), Gadalla (*Historical Deception, Tut-Ankh-Amen*), Edwards, Neubert

Twt-Ankh-Amen's Father – Osman (*The House of the Messiah*), Gadalla (*Historical Deception, Tut-Ankh-Amen*), Edwards, Neubert

The Biblical Jesus' Father – Osman (*The House of the Messiah*), Gadalla (*Historical Deception, Tut-Ankh-Amen*), Bible

Twt-Ankh-Amen's Mother – Osman (*The House of the Messiah*), Gadalla (*Historical Deception, Tut-Ankh-Amen*)

The Biblical Jesus' Mother – Osman (*The House of the Messiah*), Gadalla (*Historical Deception, Tut-Ankh-Amen*), Bible

Twt-Ankh-Amen's Consort – Osman (*The House of the Messiah*), Gadalla (*Historical Deception, Tut-Ankh-Amen*)

The Biblical Jesus' Consort – Osman (*The House of the Messiah*), Gadalla (*Historical Deception, Tut-Ankh-Amen*), Bible

Chapter 8: The Divided Kingdom

The Biblical Jesus–The King – Osman (*The House of the Mes-*

Diodorus, Gadalla (*Egyptian Mystics, Egyptian Romany, Egyptian Cosmology*), Harpur, Plutarch

Chapter 12: The Way of Horus/Christ

Bible, Budge (*Egyptian Religion, Gods I, Gods II, Egyptian Resurrection*), Campbell, Cott, Gadalla (*Egyptian Divinities, Egyptian Cosmology, Egyptian Mystics, Historical Deception, Tut-Ankh-Amen, Exiled Egyptians, Egyptian Romany*), Harpur, Kennedy, Massey, Osman (*Out of Egypt*), Pagels, Plutarch

Chapter 13: Genesis (The Mutilated Ancient Egyptian Cosmology)

The Orderly Creation Process – Bible, Budge (*Gods I & II*), Cott, Gadalla (*Egyptian Cosmology, Egyptian Mystics, Egyptian Divinities, Historical Deception, Tut-Ankh-Amen*), Pagels

In the Beginning – Bible, Budge, Cott, Gadalla (*Egyptian Cosmology, Egyptian Divinities*)

The Word – Bible, Gadalla (*Egyptian Cosmology*)

The Six Days of Creation – Bible, Budge (*Gods I & II*), Cott, Gadalla (*Egyptian Cosmology, Egyptian Mystics, Egyptian Divinities, Historical Deception, Tut-Ankh-Amen*), Pagels

The Angels of God – Gadalla (*Historical Deception, Egyptian Romany*), Osman (*House of the Messiah*)

Trinities in Ancient Egypt – Gadalla (*Egyptian Cosmology, Historical Deception, Tut-Ankh-Amen*)

Chapter 14: The Ancient Egyptian/Christian Holidays

Blackman, Catholic Encyclopedia, Diodorus, Erman, Gadalla (*Egyptian Mystics, Egyptian Romany*), Greek Orthodox website, Herodotus, Plutarch

TRF PUBLICATIONS

Tehuti Research Foundation (T.R.F.) is a non-profit, international organization, dedicated to Ancient Egyptian studies. Our books are engaging, factual, well researched, practical, interesting, and appealing to the general public. Visit our website at:

https://www.egypt-tehuti.org
E-mail address: info@egypt-tehuti.org

The publications listed below are authored by T.R.F. chairman, Moustafa Gadalla.

The publications are divided into three categories:

[I] Current Publications in English Language
[II] Earlier Available Editions in English Language
[III] Current Translated Publications in Non English Languages[Chinese, Dutch, Egyptian(so-called "arabic"), French,German, Hindi, Italian, Japanese, Portuguese, Russian & Spanish]

[I] Current Publications in English Language

Please note that printed editions of all books listed below are to be found at www.amazon.com

The Untainted Egyptian Origin—Why Ancient Egypt Matters

ISBN-13(pdf): 978-1-931446-50-1
ISBN-13(e-book): 9781931446-66-2

This book is intended to provide a short concise overview of some aspects of the Ancient Egyptian civilization that can serve us well nowadays in our daily life no matter where we are in this world. The book covers matters such as self empowerment, improvements to present political, social, economical and environmental issues, recognition and implementations of harmonic principles in our works and actions, etc.

The Ancient Egyptian Culture Revealed, Expanded 2*nd* ed.

ISBN-13(pdf): 978-1-931446-66-2
ISBN-13(e-book): 978-1-931446-65-5
ISBN-13(pbk.): 978-1-931446-67-9

This new expanded edition reveals several aspects of the Ancient Egyptian culture, such as the very remote antiquities of Egypt; the Egyptian characteristics and religious beliefs and practices; their social/political system; their cosmic temples; the richness of their language; musical heritage and comprehensive sciences; their advanced medicine; their vibrant economy; excellent agricultural and manufactured products; their transportation system; and much more.

Isis : The Divine Female

ISBN-13(pdf): 978-1-931446-25-9
ISBN-13(e-book): 978-1-931446- 26-6
ISBN-13(pbk.): 978-1-931446-31-0

This book explains the divine female principle as the source of creation (both metaphysically and physically); the feminine dual nature of Isis with Nephthys; the relationship (and one-ness) of the female and male principles; the numerology of Isis and

Osiris; Isis' role as the Virgin Mother; explanation of about twenty female deities as the manifestations of the feminine attributes; the role of Isis' ideology throughout the world; the allegory of Isis, Osiris and Horus; and much more. This book will fill both the mind with comprehensive information as well as the heart with the whole spectrum of emotions.

Egyptian Cosmology, The Animated Universe, Expanded 3rd edition

ISBN-13(pdf): 978-1-931446-44-0
ISBN-13(e-book): 978-1-931446-46-4
ISBN-13(pbk.): 978-1-931446-48-8

This new expanded edition surveys the applicability of Egyptian cosmological concepts to our modern understanding of the nature of the universe, creation, science, and philosophy. Egyptian cosmology is humanistic, coherent, comprehensive, consistent, logical, analytical, and rational. Discover the Egyptian concept of the universal energy matrix and the creation process accounts. Read about numerology, dualities,trinities, numerical significance of individual numbers thru the number ten; how the human being is related to the universe; the Egyptian astronomical consciousness; the earthly voyage; how the social and political structures were a reflection of the universe; the cosmic role of the pharaoh; and the interactions between earthly living and other realms; climbing the heavenly ladder to reunite with the Source; and more.

Egyptian Alphabetical Letters of Creation Cycle

ISBN-13(pdf): 978-1-931446-89-1
ISBN-13(e-book): 978-1-931446-88-4
ISBN-13(pbk.): 978-1-931446-87-7

This book focuses on the relationship between the sequence of the creation cycle and the Egyptian ABGD alphabets; the principles and principals of Creation; the cosmic manifestation of the Egyptian alphabet; the three primary phases of the creation cycle and their numerical values; and the creation theme of each of the three primary phases, as well as an individual analysis of each of the 28 ABGD alphabetical letters that covers each letter's role in the Creation Cycle, its sequence significance, its sound and writing form significance, its numerical significance, its names & meanings thereof, as well as its peculiar properties and its nature/impact/influence.

Egyptian Mystics: Seekers of the Way, Expanded 2nd ed.

ISBN-13(pdf): 978-1-931446-53-2
ISBN-13(e-book): 978-1-931446-54-9
ISBN-13(pbk.): 978-1-931446-55-6

This new expanded edition explains how Ancient Egypt is the origin of alchemy and present-day Sufism, and how the mystics of Egypt camouflage their practices with a thin layer of Islam. The book also explains the progression of the mystical Way towards enlightenment, with a coherent explanation of its fundamentals and practices. It includes details of basic training practices; samples of Ancient Present Egyptian festivals; the role of Isis as the 'Model Philosopher'.It shows the correspondence between the Ancient Egyptian calendar of events and the cosmic cycles of the universe; and other related miscellaneous items.

Egyptian Divinities: The All Who Are THE ONE, Expanded 2nd ed.

ISBN-13(pdf): 978-1-931446-57-0
ISBN-13(e-book): 978-1-931446-58-7
ISBN-13(pbk.): 978-1-931446-59-4

This new expanded edition shows how the Egyptian concept of God is based on recognizing the multiple attributes of the Divine. The book details more than 100 divinities (gods/goddesses); how they act and interact to maintain the universe; and how they operate in the human being—As Above so Below, and As Below so Above.It includes details of the manifestations of the neteru (gods, goddesses) in the creation process; narrations of their manifestations; man as the universal replica; the most common animals and birds neteru; and additional male and female deities.

The Ancient Egyptian Roots of Christianity, 2nd ed.

ISBN-13(pdf): 978-1-931446-75-4
ISBN-13(e-book): 978-1-931446-76-1
ISBN-13(pbk.): 978-1-931446-77-8

This new expanded edition reveals the Ancient Egyptian roots of Christianity, both historically and spiritually. This book demonstrates that the accounts of the "historical Jesus" are based entirely on the life and death of the Egyptian Pharaoh, Twt/Tut-Ankh-Amen; and that the "Jesus of Faith" and the Christian tenets are all Egyptian in origin—such as the essence of the teachings/message, as well as the religious holidays.It also demonstrates that the major biblical ancestors of the biblical Jesus—being David, Solomon and Moses are all Ancient Egyptian pharaohs as well as a comparison between the creation of the universe and man (according to the Book of Genesis) and the Ancient Egyptian creation accounts.

The Egyptian Pyramids Revisited, Expanded Third Edition

ISBN-13(pdf): 978-1-931446-79-2
ISBN-13(e-book): 978-1-931446-80-8
ISBN-13(pbk.): 978-1-931446-81-5

The new expanded edition provides complete information about the pyramids of Ancient Egypt in the Giza Plateau. It contains the locations and dimensions of interiors and exteriors of these pyramids; the history and builders of the pyramids; theories of construction; theories on their purpose and function; the sacred geometry that was incorporated into the design of the pyramids; and much, much more. It also includes details of the interiors and exteriors of the Saqqara's Zoser Stepped "Pyramid" as well as the three Snefru Pyramids that were built prior to the Giza Pyramids. It also discusses the "Pyramid Texts" and the works of the great pharaohs who followed the pharaohs of the Pyramid Age.

The Ancient Egyptian Metaphysical Architecture, Expanded Edition

ISBN-13(pdf): 978-1-931446-63-1
ISBN-13(e-book): 978-1-931446-62-4
ISBN-13(pbk): 978-1-931446-61-7

This new expanded edition reveals the Ancient Egyptian knowledge of harmonic proportion, sacred geometry, and number mysticism as manifested in their texts, temples, tombs, art, hieroglyphs, etc., throughout their known history. It shows how the Egyptians designed their buildings to generate cosmic energy; and the mystical application of numbers in Egyptian works. The book explains in detail the harmonic proportion of about 20 Ancient Egyptian buildings throughout their recorded history.It also includes additional discussions and details of the symbolism on the walls; the interactions between humans and the divine forces; Egyptian tombs, shrines and housing; as well as several miscellaneous related items.

Sacred Geometry and Numerology,

ISBN-13(e-book): 978-1-931446-23-5

This document is an introductory course for learning the fundamentals of sacred geometry and numerology, in its true and complete form, as practiced in the Egyptian traditions.

The Egyptian Hieroglyph Metaphysical Language

ISBN-13(pdf): 978-1-931446-95-2
ISBN-13(e-book): 978-1-931446-96-9
ISBN-13(pbk.): 978-1-931446-97-6

This book covers the Egyptian Hieroglyph metaphysical language of images/pictures; the language of the mind/intellect/divine; the scientific/metaphysical realities of pictorial images (Hieroglyphs) as the ultimate medium for the human consciousness that interpret, process and maintain the meanings of such images; how each hieroglyphic image has imitative and symbolic (figurative and allegorical) meanings; the concurrence of modern science of such multiple meanings of each image; how Egyptian hieroglyphic images represent metaphysical concepts; and the metaphysical significance of a variety of about 80 Egyptian Hieroglyphic images.

The Ancient Egyptian Universal Writing Modes

ISBN-13(pdf): 978-1-931446-91-4
ISBN-13(e-book): 978-1-931446-92-1
ISBN-13(pbk.): 978-1-931446-93-8

This book will show how the Egyptians had various modes of writings for various purposes, and how the Egyptian modes were falsely designated as "separate languages" belonging to others; the falsehood of having different languages on the Rosetta (and numerous other similar) Stone; and evaluation of the 'hieratic' and "demotic" forms of writing. The book will also highlight how the Egyptian alphabetical language is the MOTHER and origin of all languages (as confirmed by all writers of antiquities) and how this one original language came to be called Greek, Hebrew, Arabic and other 'languages' throughout the world through the deterioration of sound values via 'sound shifts', as well as foreign degradation of the original Egyptian writing forms.

The Enduring Ancient Egyptian Musical System—Theory and Practice, Expanded Second Edition

ISBN-13(pdf): 978-1-931446-69-3
ISBN-13(e-book): 978-1-931446-70-9
ISBN-13(pbk.): 978-1-931446-71-6

This new expanded edition explains the cosmic roots of Egyptian musical and vocal rhythmic forms. Learn the fundamentals (theory and practice) of music in the typical Egyptian way: simple, coherent, and comprehensive.It provides discussions and details of an inventory of Ancient Egyptian musical instruments explaining their ranges and playing techniques. It also discusses Egyptian rhythmic dancing and musical harmonic practices by the Ancient Egyptians and other miscellaneous items.

Egyptian Musical Instruments, 2nd ed.

ISBN-13(pdf): 978-1-931446-47-1
ISBN-13(e-book): 978-1-931446-73-0
ISBN-13(pbk.): 978-1-931446-74-7

This book presents the major Ancient Egyptian musical instruments, their ranges, and playing techniques.

The Musical Aspects of the Ancient Egyptian Vocalic Language

ISBN-13(pdf): 978-1-931446-83-9

ISBN-13(e-book): 978-1-931446-84-6
ISBN-13(pbk.): 978-1-931446-85-3

This book will show that the fundamentals, structure, formations, grammar, and syntax are exactly the same in music and in the Egyptian alphabetical language. The book will show the musical/tonal/tonic Egyptian alphabetical letters as being derived from the three primary tonal sounds/vowels; the fundamentals of generative phonology; and the nature of the four sound variations of each letter and their exact equivalence in musical notes; the generative nature of both the musical triads and its equivalence in the Egyptian trilateral stem verbs; utilization of alphabetical letters and the vocalic notations for both texts and musical instruments performance; and much more.

Egyptian Romany: The Essence of Hispania, Expanded 2nd ed.

ISBN-13(pdf.): 978-1-931446-43-3
ISBN-13(e-book): 978-1-931446- 90-7
ISBN-13(pbk.): 978-1-931446-94-5

This new expanded edition reveals the Ancient Egyptian roots of the Romany (Gypsies) and how they brought about the civilization and orientalization of Hispania over the past 6,000 years. The book shows also the intimate relationship between Egypt and Hispania archaeologically, historically, culturally, ethnologically, linguistically, etc. as a result of the immigration of the Egyptian Romany (Gypsies) to Iberia.It alsp provides discussions and details of the mining history of Iberia; the effects of Assyrians and Persians attacks on Ancient Egypt and the corresponding migrations to Iberia; the overrated "Romans" influence in Iberia; and other miscellaneous items.

[II] Earlier Available Editions in English Language — continue to be available in PDF Format

Historical Deception: The Untold Story of Ancient Egypt, 2nd ed.

ISBN-13: 978-1-931446- 09-1

Reveals the ingrained prejudices against Ancient Egypt from major religious groups and Western academicians.

Tut-Ankh-Amen: The Living Image of the Lord

ISBN-13: 978-1-931446- 12-1

The identification of the "historical Jesus" as that of the Egyptian Pharaoh, Twt/Tut-Ankh-Amen.

Exiled Egyptians: The Heart of Africa

ISBN-13: 978-1-931446-10-5

A concise and comprehensive historical account of Egypt and sub-Sahara Africa for the last 3,000 years.

The Twilight of Egypt

ISBN-13: 978-1-931446-24-2

A concise and comprehensive historical account of Egypt and the Egyptians for the last 3,000 years.

[III] Current Translated Publications in Non English Languages [Chinese, Dutch, Egyptian (so-called "arabic"), French,German, Hindi, Italian, Japanese, Portuguese, Russian & Spanish]

Details of All Translated Publications are to be found on our website

---

Made in the USA
Middletown, DE
11 July 2021